The Cycle of Juvenile Justice

THE CYCLE
OF JUVENILE
JUSTICE

Thomas J. Bernard

New York   Oxford
OXFORD UNIVERSITY PRESS
1992

Oxford University Press

Oxford   New York   Toronto
Delhi   Bombay   Calcutta   Madras   Karachi
Petaling Jaya   Singapore   Hong Kong   Tokyo
Nairobi   Dar es Salaam   Cape Town
Melbourne   Auckland

and associated companies in
Berlin   Ibadan

Published by Oxford University Press, Inc.
198 Madison Avenue, New York, New York 10016-4314

Library of Congress Cataloging-in-Publication Data
Bernard, Thomas J.
The cycle of juvenile justice /
Thomas J. Bernard.
p. cm. Includes index.
ISBN 978-0-19-507183-2
1. Juvenile justice, Administration of—History.
2. Juvenile justice, Administration of—United States—History.
I. Title. HV9065.B47 1992 364.3'6'09—dc20 91-10966

Printed in the United States of America
on acid-free paper

Contents

The Cycle of Juvenile Justice

1

Ideas and the Cycle of Juvenile Justice

The Cycle of Juvenile Justice

There is a cyclical pattern in juvenile justice policies in which the same sequence of policies has been repeated three times in the last two hundred years.[1] Present juvenile justice policies can be explained by this cycle and future changes in these policies predicted by it.[2] The specific sequence of policies in the cycle is described in Table 1.

The cycle begins at a time when justice officials and the general public are convinced that juvenile crime is at an exceptionally high level, and there are many harsh punishments but few lenient treatments for juvenile offenders. In this situation, justice officials often are forced to choose between harshly punishing juvenile offenders and doing nothing at all. As a consequence, many minor offenders are let off scot-free because lenient treatments are not available and because justice officials believe that the harsh punishments will make the minor offenders worse.

Eventually, justice officials and the general public conclude that the "forced choice" between harsh punishments and doing nothing at all is part of the problem. That is, they come to believe that harsh punishment actually increases juvenile crime, and that doing nothing at all increases it too. The solution is to introduce lenient treatments for juvenile offenders. A major reform of juvenile justice policies accomplishes this task, and everyone is optimistic that juvenile crime rates will soon decline.

3

TABLE 1. The Cycle of Juvenile Justice

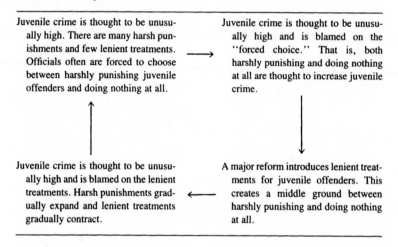

Juvenile crime is thought to be unusually high. There are many harsh punishments and few lenient treatments. Officials often are forced to choose between harshly punishing juvenile offenders and doing nothing at all. → Juvenile crime is thought to be unusually high and is blamed on the "forced choice." That is, both harshly punishing and doing nothing at all are thought to increase juvenile crime.

Juvenile crime is thought to be unusually high and is blamed on the lenient treatments. Harsh punishments gradually expand and lenient treatments gradually contract. ← A major reform introduces lenient treatments for juvenile offenders. This creates a middle ground between harshly punishing and doing nothing at all.

But both justice officials and the general public remain convinced that juvenile crime is at an exceptionally high level. After some time, they begin to blame lenient treatments for the high crime rates. Initially, responses to serious juvenile offenders are "toughened up," so that those offenders receive harsh punishments rather than lenient treatments. The responses for average or typical juvenile offenders are also "toughened up" so that they too receive harsh punishments. This process continues until there are many harsh punishments available for responding to juvenile offenders but few lenient treatments. At that point, justice officials and the general public remain convinced that juvenile crime is at an exceptionally high level and justice officials often are forced to choose between harshly punishing juvenile offenders and doing nothing at all. The cycle has returned to where it started.

Ideas Drive the Cycle

At every stage of the cycle, justice officials and the general public believe three ideas: that juvenile crime is at an exceptionally high level, that present juvenile justice policies make the problem worse, and that changing those policies will reduce juvenile crime. These people usually believe that their ideas are new and different, but in fact they have been continuously believed for at least two hundred years. These ideas drive us from one policy to the next as we pursue a lower level of juvenile crime.

Two other ideas change as the cycle moves from policy to policy. These are called *ideas of juvenile delinquency* and *ideas of juvenile justice*. An idea of juvenile delinquency is a general overview of what delinquency is and how it originates. The idea does not have to be very specific and it does not have to explain all delinquency. For example, one person might think that delinquency in general is criminal behavior committed by juveniles who care only about themselves, not about the rights of other people. Another person regards delinquency as a cry for help from juveniles in neglecting or abusive environments.

Each person can be expected to have an idea of juvenile justice that is associated with their idea of juvenile delinquency. The first person probably would favor policies that punish juveniles in proportion to the offense that they committed. The second person probably would favor policies that respond to the juvenile's cry for help either by aiding the juvenile directly or by addressing the neglecting and abusive social environments in which the juvenile lives.

Reforms of the juvenile justice system can be phrased in terms of these two types of ideas. The idea of juvenile justice is the reform itself: it provides a brief and readily understandable image of the policies the reformer wants to implement. The idea of juvenile delinquency explains why the reformer thinks the new policy will work. It does this by proposing a simple image of the kind of people delinquents are. If delinquents really are the way the reformer describes, then the proposed policy will work when it is put into practice. If, however, delinquents are quite different, then the new policy will not work and may even make the problem of delinquency worse.

For example, those who favor punishment and deterrence policies (an idea of juvenile justice) typically describe delinquents as criminals who care only for their own well-being and do not care about the rights of others (an idea of juvenile delinquency). If this idea of juvenile delinquency is correct, then punishment and deterrence policies probably will reduce delinquency, but reform and rehabilitation policies probably will have no effect and might even make the problem worse. If, however, delinquency is a cry for help from victims of neglecting and abusive environments (a contrasting idea of juvenile delinquency), then punishment and deterrence policies probably will have no effect and might even

make the problem worse, while reform and rehabilitation policies probably will reduce delinquency.

Organization of This Book

We can establish a stable and reasonable juvenile justice policy only by
breaking out of the cycle of juvenile justice. More than anything else, that
requires that we change our ideas about juvenile delinquency and juvenile
justice: the three ideas that remain the same and the two ideas that change
as the cycle of juvenile justice goes from policy to policy.[3] Changing
those ideas is the overall goal of this book.

Chapter 2 examines the general role of ideas in history, philosophy,
and law, which forms the general framework for the discussion of the
cycle of juvenile justice. I also define the question that organizes the next
four chapters in this book: "What aspects of juvenile delinquency and
juvenile justice have stayed the same for at least two hundred years, and
what aspects have changed in that period?"

Chapter 3 looks at the aspects of juvenile delinquency and juvenile
justice that have stayed the same for at least two hundred years. Five
unchanging aspects are identified, although the public generally believes
that each has changed in the recent past. These five unchanging aspects
lead to a sixth: the cycle of juvenile justice itself.

Chapter 4 is the first of five chapters that examines aspects of juvenile
delinquency and juvenile justice that have changed in the last two
hundred years. It makes the controversial argument that juvenile delinquency itself is one of those aspects: the behaviors we typically describe
as juvenile delinquency first appeared in the United States and Western
Europe around the year 1800. This "modern phenomenon of juvenile
delinquency" arose because of urbanization, industrialization, and the
breakdown of traditional controls. This same modern phenomenon later
appeared in other places in the world as those places underwent the same
processes of "modernization."

A new way of understanding and interpreting offensive behavior by
young people also originated around the year 1800. This was the idea that
juvenile delinquents were "potential paupers." Chapter 5 discusses how
this "idea of juvenile delinquency" formed the basis for a new "idea of
juvenile justice": the first juvenile institution was established in New
York in 1825.

In actual practice, juvenile institutions failed to solve the problem of delinquency. Ultimately, the idea that delinquents were potential paupers was replaced by a new idea that delinquents were dependent and neglected children. This "idea of juvenile delinquency" formed the basis for a new "idea of juvenile justice": the first juvenile court was established in Chicago in 1899. Chapter 6 discusses the founding of this court, and concludes by describing seven "lessons of history" that are consistent with the history of juvenile delinquency and juvenile justice up to this point.

Chapter 7 focuses on a series of decisions by the United States Supreme Court that form the philosophical and legal basis for juvenile justice policy today. These decisions essentially express our "good intentions" with respect to the juvenile justice system, but they appear strangely out of place with respect to the "lessons of history" derived at the end of Chapter 6. If those lessons are correct, then it would seem likely that Supreme Court decisions have not influenced the actual practice of juvenile justice to any great degree.

Chapter 8 looks at the actual practice of juvenile justice today, and finds that the Supreme Court decisions have not been implemented. Rather, juvenile justice policy is largely determined by the ideas of the "get tough" movement. This movement argues that juvenile delinquents are serious criminals. This "idea of juvenile delinquency" forms the basis for an "idea of juvenile justice": swift, certain, and severe punishments for youthful offenders. These ideas and policies are consistent with the lessons of history as presented at the end of Chapter 6, and therefore support the conclusion that the lessons themselves are valid.

Chapter 9 uses those lessons of history to predict future developments in juvenile justice policy. I predict that the cycle of juvenile justice will simply continue and that we will repeat the mistakes of the past rather than learn from it. This will lead to a fairly specific sequence of events quite likely to occur over the next twenty or thirty years.

Despite my pessimism about our ability to break the cycle of juvenile justice, I suggest ways to learn from the past rather than merely repeat it. I suggest an "idea of juvenile delinquency" as naive risk-taking, and an "idea of juvenile justice" as communication that actions have consequences. These ideas are derived from the actual functioning of the juvenile justice system at the present time, and I believe that they could form the basis for a stable juvenile justice policy. However, I also conclude they have little chance of being implemented because they are so inconsistent with the lessons of history described in Chapter 6.

Even if we cannot "solve" the problem of delinquency, I argue in Chapter 10 that delinquency will someday "end." Juvenile delinquency originated as a modern phenomenon in response to changes in the larger society, including urbanization, industrialization, and the breakdown of traditional controls. As societies continue to change, the modern phenomenon of juvenile delinquency eventually will pass away.

In the meantime, I hope that we admit that juvenile delinquency is not simply a product of evil and inferior youths. The modern problem of delinquency did not emerge around the year 1800 because juveniles themselves suddenly changed, but because the societal context in which juveniles found themselves suddenly changed. That change occurred for many good reasons, the most important of which was that it vastly increased the wealth of the larger society. That change was not without unwanted side effects, however; one was the modern problem of juvenile delinquency.

I believe that fairness requires us to choose kinder, gentler policies for responding to delinquents. The cruel and harsh policies favored today are only one stage in the cycle of juvenile justice. Past experience suggests that these policies will fail and that they eventually will be abandoned as the cycle of juvenile justice moves to its next stage.

These harsh policies are based on an illusion that delinquency is a problem that can be solved. That illusion has been extremely costly in human and financial terms. Let us abandon these policies now, since we will eventually abandon them in the future anyway. Let us instead adopt fair and reasonable policies that respond to delinquency as a continuing presence in modern society. We cannot ignore the dangers of delinquency, but neither should we ignore the fact that our own choices play a central role in creating and maintaining this problem.

Notes

1. A similar analysis of cycles in juvenile justice can be found in Theodore N. Ferdinand, "Juvenile Delinquency or Juvenile Justice: Which Came First?" *Criminology* 27(1):79–106. Both Ferdinand and I argue that there were increases in the rates and seriousness of delinquency at the time of the origin of juvenile justice, but Ferdinand attributes those increases to the juvenile justice system itself while I attribute them to

urbanization, industrialization, and the breakdown of traditional controls. Both Ferdinand and I agree that reforms initially were directed toward minor offenders and gradually applied to more serious offenders over time. Both of us agree that the impetus for the reform comes when officials face the choice between harsh punishments and doing nothing at all. Ferdinand, however, argues that each successive reform widens the net by ''embracing ever more normal populations,'' whereas I depict a cycle in which minor offenders are brought into the system with the reform, gradually excluded from it as the system turns its attention to serious offenders, and then brought back into it with the next reform. For an analysis of cycles in this century, see J. Lawrence Schultz, ''The Cycle of Juvenile Court History,'' *Crime and Delinquency* 19:457–76 (Oct., 1973). Analyses that are consistent with a cyclical pattern can be found in James O. Finkenauer, *The Panacea Solution*, Prentice-Hall, Englewood Cliffs, NJ, 1981, and John R. Sutton, *Stubborn Children*, University of California Press, Berkeley, 1988. For a more general argument about cycles related to juvenile justice and focused on more recent times, see James Gilbert, *A Cycle of Outrage*, Oxford, New York, 1986.

2. A more detailed description of the cycle is found on pp. 105–6 below. Predictions about future changes in juvenile justice policy are found on pp. 155–56 below.

3. While I argue that juvenile justice policy is the product of cultural or ideological factors, I also argue that juvenile delinquency is the product of structural factors, including urbanization, industrialization, and the breakdown of the traditional structural controls associated with peasant and feudal societies. See the discussion of the origin of juvenile delinquency in Chapter 3 and the end of juvenile delinquency in Chapter 10.

2

Ideas in History, Philosophy, and Law

Ideas of juvenile delinquency and juvenile justice drive the cycle of juvenile justice. These ideas emerge at certain points in *history*, and reflect the historical conditions in existence at the time. The ideas are elaborated into *philosophies*, in the sense of rational, coherent, and organized ways of understanding and interpreting the world. The philosophies then form the basis for *laws* that define juvenile delinquency, establish the juvenile justice system, and determine juvenile justice policies. Thus, juvenile delinquency and juvenile justice can only be understood by studying ideas in the context of history, philosophy, and law.

Ideas in History

Many students view history as a large and uninteresting pile of information about what happened in the past that they are expected to memorize and repeat on a test. In fact, the main reason for studying the past is to better understand the *present* and the *future*. That is the purpose of this examination of the history of juvenile delinquency and juvenile justice.

History as Context

Imagine a fish swimming in water. There is a sense in which the fish does not see the water—rather, the water is its whole world. Now imagine yourself standing on a dock looking down at that fish. Because you are outside of the water, you see both the fish and the water it swims in. There is a sense in which you understand the fish's world better than the fish because you can look at it from the outside.

We too are like fish: we "swim" in our historical context the way the fish swims in water. Someone standing outside our historical context can observe us within it, just as we can see the fish in the water. But we normally have no sense of our own context—to us, it is the whole world.

Studying history is one way to get "outside" our historical context, and thus gain a perspective on it. Looked at in that way, studying history does not mean memorizing information about some distant time and place. Instead, it means becoming immersed in a different historical context, just as if the fish suddenly were to jump out of the water and stand on the dock with you. Once you have "swum" in a different context, you can go back to your own context and view it with new eyes. You acquire a new understanding of the world in which you live.

Understanding the present is not the only reason to study history— there is also the future. The philosopher Santayana said: "Those who do not know history are condemned to repeat it."[1] If we could learn from the past, we could save ourselves a lot of time and trouble in the future.

The Past as Convenient or Inconvenient in the Present

The past always implies lessons about the present and the future, so people often have reasons in the present for their beliefs about the past. People want to believe things about the past that support their views of the present and the future. Thus, many people have strong opinions about the past even when they have little information about it.

I use the term "myth" to describe beliefs about the past that are strongly held and convenient to believe but are based on little actual information.[2] Myths are not necessarily false—people generally just don't know or care whether they are true or false. They hold the belief because it is convenient to do so.

The history of delinquency is a subject about which people sometimes have strong beliefs but little information. There may be reasons in the present why people hold these beliefs about the past. For example, consider the following three beliefs about the history of delinquency. Think about them as "myths" rather than actual stories of what happened in the past. That is, think about what they imply about the present and the future, and why they might be convenient or inconvenient for you to believe:

1. Delinquency in the past was much more serious than it is today (the myth of progress).
2. Delinquency in the past was about the same as it is today (the myth that nothing changes).
3. Delinquency in the past was much less serious than it is today (the myth of the good old days).

Not many people believe the first "myth" regarding juvenile delinquency—that delinquency in the past was worse than it is today. For some reason, this myth suggests lessons about the present and the future that most people do not want to believe. Perhaps it leaves people feeling vulnerable: if we believe this, we might let our guard down in the present and could be overwhelmed by a flood of juvenile crime in the future. Better to always believe that things are terrible than to be fooled even once.

I might mention that, at least for the recent past, this "myth" is clearly true. Delinquency today is a less serious problem than it was fifteen or twenty years ago. A discussion of this topic can be found in Chapter 3.

More people believe the second "myth"—that delinquency does not change over time. People who believe this feel comfortable with the view that delinquency always has been here and always will be because it is a part of human nature. If this myth were true, there would be no point in studying delinquency from a historical perspective because it always has been pretty much as it is now.

This myth is false because delinquency has changed greatly over time. I already mentioned that delinquency is a less serious problem today than it was fifteen or twenty years ago. I will also argue that the "modern" form of juvenile delinquency originated around the year 1800, and it was a very different phenomenon before that time (see Chapter 4). Thus, the myth that delinquency remains the same over time is clearly false.

Even though it is false, this myth about the past can be convenient to believe in the present. For example, if delinquency is more or less the same at all times and places, then it cannot be caused by particular characteristics of our own society such as poverty, inequality, unemployment, racial discrimination, urban slums, poor schools, and so on. This means, in order to solve the problem of delinquency, we do not have to solve those social problems with programs that would be difficult and expensive (i.e., inconvenient).

The third "myth" is probably held by more people than the first two "myths" combined. This is the myth of the good old days: "Things today are worse than they ever were in the past. Why, back in the good old days, kids respected their parents and the worst thing they did was to skip school and steal candy from the corner store."

Most people who hold this belief suggest that the "good old days" were thirty or forty years ago, not several hundred or several thousand years ago. That is, the "good old days" were back when the present generation of adults were young. Today, for example, the "good old days" would be the 1940s and 1950s.

The myth of the "good old days" is true some of the time and false some of the time. Delinquency does not remain the same all the time (as the second "myth" would have it), so there are times when there is more delinquency and times when there is less. At times when there is more delinquency, then there really were some "good old days" when there was less delinquency.

But even when this is true, it is still a "myth" because people tend to believe it without any particular concern about whether it is true. People always like to believe in the "good old days," whether delinquency was actually better or worse back then.

There may be reasons in the present why people prefer to believe this "myth" about the past. There is a sense in which this myth is much more optimistic than either of the other two myths. If delinquency really was not a serious problem thirty or forty years ago, then we can solve the problem of delinquency today by doing what they were doing back then. For example, perhaps delinquency was punished more severely then than it is now: "Why, back in the good old days, when kids acted up, you got all over them like a wet blanket. There was no coddling of criminals, like there is today."

The "myth of the good old days" is optimistic because it implies that a relatively simple and available solution to the problem of delinquency exists. Everyone prefers to believe that problems like delinquency can be quickly and completely solved if only certain clear and simple steps are taken. That is so much more appealing than believing that the problems require difficult, time-consuming, and costly measures that will be only partially effective.

People tend to believe the myth of the good old days all of the time, but it is only true some of the time. For example, in the 1940s and 1950s (the "good old days" of today), many people believed that there was a wave of serious delinquency caused by the leniency of punishments at that time. They also believed that delinquency was not a serious problem back in the "good old days," which at the time were the 1910s and 1920s.

The myth of the good old days is a constant in history and forms a central element in the cycle of juvenile justice. At any given time, people are convinced that they are in the middle of a juvenile crime wave and that juvenile crime was not a serious problem only thirty or forty years ago. This leads them to believe that certain clear and simple steps can solve the problem of delinquency. The cycle itself is formed out of the sequence of steps that are taken.

What Stays the Same and What Changes?

An honest look at history would try to determine what actually happened in the past, and only then decide what it means for us in the present and the future. That will be my attempt in this book although, like everyone else, I could have biases that affect my views without my knowing it.

The particular way in which I attempt to take an honest look at history is to ask the question: "What has stayed the same in the past and what has changed?" My purpose in asking this question is to understand the present and future. I assume that whatever has changed in the past can change again in the future, and whatever has stayed the same in the past probably will stay the same in the future. Thus, the question is intended to establish a baseline for what we can and cannot expect from juvenile justice policy in the present and future.

The more precise question I ask is as follows: What aspects of juvenile delinquency and juvenile justice have stayed the same for at least two hundred years (i.e., since the late 1700s), and what aspects have changed during that period? If there are aspects of juvenile delinquency and juvenile justice that have not changed for at least two hundred years, then I will infer that those aspects are not likely to change in response to new and different policies that we might implement, even if those policies seem to make a great deal of sense to us. On the other hand, if there are aspects of juvenile delinquency and juvenile justice that have changed in the last two hundred years, then I will infer that these aspects might change again in the future under the proper conditions. If we wish further change, then we should attempt to understand the conditions under which the earlier change took place. Once we understand that, then we can decide whether we want to attempt to create the conditions for further change in the future.

Ideas in Philosophy

For many students, about the only thing that is even more useless than history is philosophy. It seems especially useless in a practical endeavor such as the juvenile justice system, where we are trying to reduce predatory and violent crimes by juveniles in our society. The important thing is what works, not how you look at it.

In contrast, I will argue that philosophical views are extremely important for understanding juvenile delinquency and the juvenile justice system. "Philosophy," in the sense that I use the term, refers to organized sets of ideas through which we interpret and understand the world. In general, these sets of ideas are logical, coherent, and intuitively appealing. They hang together and make sense. They also generally express values about what is good and bad, right and wrong, just and unjust, appropriate and inappropriate, and important and unimportant.

Philosophy as Context

A person's philosophy is part of their "context," much like the historical context discussed above. That is, a person's philosophical views can be like the water in which the fish swims: the fish does not see the water since the water is the fish's whole world. In a similar way, people who have a particular philosophical point of view may not see that view at all, since they think they are simply seeing "the world."

If we stand on the dock looking at the fish swimming around, we see the fish in its context—that is, in the water. Similarly, if we stand outside our own philosophical context, we can get a sense of the ideas that we use to interpret and understand the world. Otherwise, we tend to believe that our way of interpreting and understanding the world is reality.

One way to get outside our philosophical context is to study history.

For example, I will argue that our way of understanding and interpreting delinquency originated around the year 1800, about the same time the modern phenomenon of delinquency emerged. If we can get a sense of this different way of interpreting and understanding what we now call "juvenile delinquency," we will be better able to comprehend our own way of interpreting and understanding this phenomenon.

Philosophical Ideas and Organizational Decision-Making

Philosophical ideas are important because the public typically demands that the juvenile justice system "make sense"—that is, be rational and coherent. You might think that all large organizations must "make sense" in the same way, so that philosophical ideas would be no more important for understanding the juvenile justice system than they would for, say, a large corporation. But the fact is no one expects large corporations to "make sense" in the way that we expect the juvenile justice system to "make sense."

For example, in our modern economy, a car or a computer may be built in four countries, assembled in a fifth, and marketed in a sixth.[3] Does this make any sense? Is this rational? Is this a reasonable way to make a product? Wouldn't it be better to do it all in one place?

Corporate executives do not care whether this way of doing things "makes sense" or whether it seems "rational" or "a reasonable way to do things." All they care about is whether it makes money. Profit is the "bottom line" for all businesses. In their pursuit of profits, corporations engage in activities that, if looked at in a purely rational way, do not seem to make any sense at all.[4] For each individual move, corporate executives issue statements that "make sense," that sound "reasonable" and "coherent." But these statements usually have little to do with the real goal, which is to achieve greater profits, especially in the short run.[5] If we were to try to understand corporate decision-making, we would not get very far by studying those statements. Philosophical ideas (in the sense of rational, coherent ideas that "hang together" and "make sense") really have little impact on corporate decisions.

Philosophical Ideas and the Juvenile Justice System

In contrast, rational, coherent ideas that "hang together" and "make sense" are extremely important for decision-making in the juvenile justice system. The public demands that juvenile justice policies "make sense" in terms of whatever philosophy they happen to hold. If they hold a conservative philosophy, then they demand that the juvenile justice system "get tough" with juveniles and punish them for their offenses. If they hold a liberal philosophy, then they demand that the juvenile justice system rehabilitate juveniles and treat the causes of their problems.

The public generally has little or no information about how well their recommended policies work, and they don't care either. They simply assume that the programs will work because they "make sense." It doesn't occur to them that programs that "make sense" might not work very well, and that programs that work very well might not "make sense."

In business, it is hard to avoid the bottom line: quarterly reports come out and you know whether your policy is increasing profits or not. In juvenile justice, it is easy to avoid the bottom line: if the results do not match up with your expectation, you throw them out. After all, no one really knows how well the juvenile justice system works anyway.

Ideas in Law

Unlike history and philosophy, law seems relevant to juvenile delinquency and juvenile justice, since it is intimately involved in both. Law defines the nature of juvenile delinquency by defining the actions that would result in the juvenile's being officially processed by the juvenile justice system. In general, delinquency is defined by two kinds of laws. First, juveniles are required to obey the same criminal laws that adults obey. This includes federal, state, and local laws. Any act that would result in a criminal prosecution if committed by an adult can result in a juvenile court hearing if committed by a juvenile. This includes serious crimes such as murder, rape, armed robbery, aggravated assault, burglary, larceny, auto theft, and arson. These can be described as *criminal offenses*.[6]

But juveniles also are required to obey a second set of laws that adults do not have to obey. These are usually called *status offenses*, since they apply only to those persons who have the status of being a juvenile. This includes laws against truancy, running away from home, refusing to obey parents, violating curfew, drinking alcohol, and engaging in consensual sexual activity. Adults are free to engage in these actions, but juveniles who do can be brought into the juvenile court and placed on probation. In the past, many youths were sent to institutions for these offenses, although fewer are today.

Law also creates the juvenile justice system, as separate from the adult criminal justice system. At the broadest level, the system itself is a product of laws, and its broadest guidelines and purposes are defined by laws. It also defines specific details about the system. In particular, it defines what the agents of the system, such as police, prosecutors, defense lawyers, judges, and probation officers, can and cannot do with, to, and for juveniles. Thus, the juvenile justice system cannot be understood apart from the law.

Law in the Context of History and Philosophy

It is helpful to study law in the context of history and philosophy, as it is presented here. Laws are rational and coherent sets of ideas that hang together and intuitively make sense. Thus, law itself is a particular form of philosophy, as defined above. It originates in "philosophical" ideas about what is good and bad, right and wrong, just and unjust, appropriate and inappropriate, and important and unimportant.

These ideas, and therefore the law, respond to historical conditions and consequently change over time. Our particular laws reflect the philosophical ideas popular in our time and can only be fully understood by studying the process by which they have evolved in response to changing historical conditions. Thus, you cannot really understand law unless you understand both the history and the philosophy behind it.

For example, the original laws that separated the juvenile courts from the adult courts were based on certain philosophical ideas that emerged in a particular historical context. It is not possible to fully understand the juvenile court we have today without understanding the context in which it appeared, and how people in that time and place understood and interpreted the world in which they lived. More recently, those ideas have changed and the laws are therefore changing along with them. To understand these changes, it is necessary to realize how the historical context has changed and how that has affected the way we understand and interpret the world.

Summary and Conclusion

This book is a history of juvenile delinquency and juvenile justice, but it is not simply a pile of dead information about the past. That is because information about the past always implies lessons about the present and the future. But most people have strong views about present and future juvenile justice policies, so most people also have strong views about the history of juvenile delinquency and juvenile justice. Thus, this book is probably going to be "lively" rather than "dead," in the sense of provoking emotional responses in its readers. After all, it is bound to support some strongly held views and threaten others.

Much of this book focuses on the various philosophies that have been the source of juvenile justice policies in the past. People demand that juvenile justice policies make sense, that they be reasonable and logical and consistent. In that sense, people demand that juvenile justice policies be based on a coherent "philosophy." At the same time, people usually have little information about whether such policies actually work. They simply assume the policies work because they make sense.

Rational and coherent ideas that "hang together" and make sense (philosophies) are joined with convenient views of what happened in the past (history) to form the basis for definitions of juvenile delinquency and policy responses to it in the juvenile justice system (laws). Laws therefore are best understood by studying them in their historical and philosophical contexts.

The cycle of juvenile justice occurs because people repeat the past rather than learn from it. We can break the cycle of juvenile justice by learning from the past, by being open to the lessons it teaches us regardless of whether those lessons support or threaten our views of the present and future. We can break the cycle of juvenile justice by learning about the actual performance of juvenile justice policies in the past, regardless of whether those policies seem rational and coherent and make sense to us.

Ultimately, we can break the cycle of juvenile justice by studying the past to get a sense of our own philosophical and historical context. Otherwise, we become immersed in our context, like a fish in water, and no longer are aware that we are in a context.

Notes

1. George Santayana, *The Life of Reason*, Constable, London, 1905, p. 284.
2. See David J. Rothman, *Conscience and Convenience*, for an analysis of how "convenience" can shape moral beliefs in general.
3. Alvin Toffler, *Powershift*, Bantam, New York, 1990.
4. E.g., see the story of "Covenant Corporation," a pseudonym for a real corporation, in Robert Jackall, *Moral Mazes*, Oxford, New York, 1988, pp. 25–32.
5. Ibid., pp. 134–61.
6. This term is not completely accurate because, as discussed in Chapter 6, juveniles cannot legally commit criminal offenses. However, the term has the advantage of being clearly understandable. The accurate term—nonstatus offenses—is unclear and confusing.

3

What Stays the Same in History?

This chapter examines aspects of juvenile delinquency and juvenile justice that have stayed the same for at least two hundred years. Some of these aspects have remained unchanged for a much longer time, even since the dawn of recorded history. This is one-half of the question being asked about history: "What aspects of juvenile delinquency and juvenile justice have stayed the same for at least two hundred years, and what aspects have changed?"

Five aspects of juvenile delinquency and juvenile justice have stayed the same for at least two hundred years:

1. Juveniles, especially young males, commit more crime than other groups.
2. There are special laws that only juveniles are required to obey.
3. Juveniles are punished less severely than adults who commit the same offenses.
4. Many people believe that the current group of juveniles commit more frequent and serious crime than juveniles in the past—that is, there is a "juvenile crime wave" at the present time.
5. Many people blame juvenile justice policies for the supposed "juvenile crime wave," arguing that they are too lenient (serious offenders laugh at "kiddie court") or that they are too harsh (minor offenders are embittered and channelled into a life of crime).

Although these five aspects have stayed the same for at least two hundred years, at each point in time people generally believed that things were different only thirty or forty years ago. Thus, these five unchanging aspects are often associated with a "myth of the good old days" and with the optimistic view that the "juvenile crime wave" would end if we only implemented the juvenile justice policies we had back then.

These five aspects give rise to a sixth aspect that has stayed the same for at least two hundred years—what I call the "cycle of juvenile justice." This cycle arises from the fact that, at any given time, many people are convinced that the problem of high juvenile crime is recent and did not exist in the "good old days." These people conclude that the problem lies in the policies for handling juvenile offenders, whether those are harsh punishments or lenient treatments. The result is a cycle of reform in which harsh punishments are blamed for high juvenile crime rates and are replaced by lenient treatments, and then lenient treatments are blamed for high juvenile crime rates and are replaced by harsh punishments.

The Behavior of Youth, Especially Young Males

Regardless of whether crime is high or low at a particular time or place, young people (and especially young males) commit a greater proportion of the crime than would be expected from their proportion in the population.[1] For example, juveniles between the ages of 13 and 17 are about 8% of the population of the United States at present.[2] If they were arrested at the same rate as everyone else, they would account about 8% of arrests. Instead, they account for almost twice as many arrests, including twice as many for serious violent crimes and almost four times as many for serious property crimes.

Recent Changes in Juvenile Crime in the United States

Prior to 1952, juvenile arrest rates in the United States were fairly low and fairly stable. In 1951, for example, juveniles accounted for 4.5% of all arrests, including 3.7% of arrests for serious violent crimes and 14.6% of arrests for serious property crimes. With some minor fluctuations, such as a temporary increase during World War II, these figures had been fairly stable at least back to the beginning of the century.[3]

While low by today's standards, juvenile crime was considered a serious problem at the time. A textbook published in 1954 included the following statement:

> Nowhere does the failure of crime control show up more clearly than among our youth. Even before World War II, according to one study, national statistics indicated that some two million of forty-three million boys and girls in the United States below the age of eighteen years came to the attention of the police annually. Youth plays a top-heavy part in the traditional crimes that feed the headlines and for which arrests are made. They frequently commit the familiar crimes against property, often with attendant violence, and their inexperience and lack of judgment make them relatively easy to apprehend.[4]

Juvenile arrests began to rise in 1952 and continued until they peaked in 1974.[5] In that year, juveniles accounted for 45% of all arrests, including 22.6% of those for serious violent crimes and 50.7% of arrests for serious property crimes. That was also the year in which the total juvenile population (i.e., everyone in the country who is younger than 18 years old) peaked at about 34 million. Since then, the juvenile population has declined to about 28 million, a decrease of about 20%.

The decline in the juvenile population has been accompanied by a decline in the proportion of arrests that involve juveniles. In 1989, juveniles accounted for 15.5% of all arrests, including 15.4% of arrests for serious violent crimes (murder, forcible rape, robbery, and aggravated assault), and 32.7% of arrests for serious property crimes (burglary, larceny-theft, motor vehicle theft, and arson). While this represents a drop of about one-third in the *proportion* of arrests that involve juveniles, the *rate* of juvenile arrests (i.e., the number of arrests adjusted for the number of juveniles in the population) has remained relatively constant.[6]

Juvenile Crime in Earlier Times

Even when juvenile arrest rates were what we now consider low, people were concerned about how much crime juveniles committed. For example, in 1938, England was alarmed by a report that found that convictions of males peaked at age 13, and that the probability of conviction was greater from ages 11 to 17 than at any other age.[7] In the United States, a report in 1940 pointed out that "young people between 15 and 21 constitute only 13% of the population above 15, but their share in the total volume of serious crime committed far exceeds their proportionate representation."[8] Extensive publicity about the "juvenile crime wave" followed in 1941 and 1942.[9] The FBI supported this publicity with statistics that showed big increases in delinquency, but the Children's Bureau, a government agency that also monitored delinquency, said that the increases were due to changes in reporting practices by police and court agencies.

These concerns are not confined to our century. In the middle of the 1800s, many young men roamed around the "Wild West" with guns strapped to their hips looking for trouble. Although stories about people like Billy the Kid were exaggerated into legends, it was still an exceptionally violent period.[10]

In the early 1800s, there were a large number of stories in the press about the extensive criminality of youth.[11] For example, a commentator on the problems of crime in London was alarmed by the volume of juvenile crime:

> It is a most extraordinary fact, that half the number of persons convicted of crime have not attained the age of discretion.[12]

About that time, there were 3,000 prisoners in London under the age of 20, half of whom were under 17 and some of whom were as young as 6.[13] These convictions were not merely for minor offenses or youthful misbehaviors. In 1785, the Solicitor-General of England stated in the House of Commons that eighteen out of twenty offenders executed in London the previous year were under the age of 21.

Gang fights are often viewed as a modern phenomenon, but Shakespeare's play *Romeo and Juliet,* set in fifteenth-century Italy, revolves around what we would now call a gang fight. The young men of the Montagu family, which included Romeo, had been in running battle with the young men of the Capulet family, which included Juliet. On a hot summer day with "the mad blood stirring," the two groups happened to run into each other on the street. In the initial exchange, a polite greeting ("Gentlemen, good day: a word with one of you") was answered by a challenge to fight ("And but one word with one of us? couple it with something: make it a word and a blow"). After a few more exchanges, the fight began and two youths, both about 16 years old, were killed.

The events in this story were placed in fifteenth-century Italy, but they could have been situated in the United States in modern times. In fact, the play and movie *West Side Story* were based on Romeo and Juliet but set in New York City in the 1950s. If the play were written for today, it might take place in Los Angeles. This illustrates that stories about the criminality of young people, and of young males in particular, are not unique to any particular time or place.

We could continue this tale back to the first crime recorded in the Bible, in which Cain (the eldest son of Adam and Eve) killed his younger brother Abel. Ever since then, young people in general, and young men in particular, have been committing crimes at a greater rate than other people. We are always aware of this phenomenon but tend to lose track of the fact that it has always been this way.

What Explains Juvenile Crime?

Why is it that young people in general, and young men in particular, commit such a large proportion of crime? Is it their biological makeup, with large volumes of hormones running through their systems? Is it their psychological state of mind, generated by the conflicts of adolescence? Is it socialization into roles, with expectations that young men will be strong and in control, but never weak or "chicken"? Various explanations of this phenomenon are presented in texts on juvenile delinquency,[14] but those explanations are not reviewed here.

For whatever reason, young people in general and young men in particular have always committed more than their share of crime. Thus, we should expect that this will continue in the future. Some people may argue that if we only implement a particular policy (e.g., death penalty, psychoanalysis, lengthy prison sentences, education, or employment training), then juveniles will stop committing more than their share of crime. The lessons of history suggest that these people are wrong.

Special Laws for Juveniles

A second aspect that has stayed the same for at least two hundred years (and seems to have remained constant over recorded history) is that certain offenses apply only to youths, not adults. At the present, these are called *status offenses,* since they only apply to people with the status of being a juvenile. The most common of these laws today are laws against running away from home, refusing to attend school (truancy), and refusing to obey parents (incorrigibility). Other common status offenses involve drinking alcoholic beverages, violating curfew, and engaging in consensual sexual activities.

Adults are allowed to do all these things, but juveniles who do the same commit punishable offenses. Adults who do not like their family can move out, but a juvenile who moves out may be arrested by the police. Adults can quit school or quit their job, but a juvenile who quits school may be taken to juvenile court and placed on probation. Adults are free to engage in most consensual sexual activities, but juveniles who engage in the same activities may be sent to a juvenile institution.

Status Offenses in Earlier Times

Originally, offenses that applied solely to youths focused on the duties that people held for their parents. In the Code of Moses in the Bible, for example, there were severe penalties including death for striking or cursing your parents,[15] although these severe punishments were rarely carried out in practice.

The Puritans made these Biblical passages the basis for a "stubborn child" law in 1646.[16] That law "served as a direct or indirect model for legislation enacted by every American state making children's misbehavior a punishable offense." It was substantially modified through the years but remained in force in Massachusetts until 1973. Since the days of the Puritans, there has been a continual expansion of attempts to control the noncriminal but "offensive" behavior of children through legal means.

Decriminalization? Deinstitutionalization?

Today, considerable debate exists about how to handle these offenses. Some people argue that the laws against these activities should be repealed: *decriminalization* of status offenses. People who favor decriminalization argue that status offenses are harmful to the youths who engage in them, but that handling these offenses in juvenile court takes a bad situation and makes it worse. They argue that voluntary social service agencies, not the juvenile court, should intervene with these youths.

Other people argue that juveniles who commit status offenses should be handled in juvenile courts but should never be locked up for such offenses. These people favor *deinstitutionalization* of status offenses. This is generally considered a more moderate response, since the offenses remain subject to the juvenile court.

In practice, however, deinstitutionalization is not much different from decriminalization. Imagine a juvenile who is brought into juvenile court for truancy, and the judge orders her to go to school. But if status offenses are "deinstitutionalized," then the judge cannot send her to an institution and can only place her on probation. If she still refuses to go to school, the judge can do nothing.

In effect, deinstitutionalizing status offenses means that the juvenile court has no power to enforce these laws. If you are going to do that, then you might as well repeal the laws—that is, decriminalize status offenses.

Status Offenses as an Aspect That Stays the Same

The lessons of history suggest that neither decriminalization or deinstitutionalization will work in the long run. Status offenses go back to the beginning of recorded history. Because this appears to be something that has stayed the same over this long span, it seems unlikely to change in the future.

In fact, in states that have decriminalized status offenses, such as Washington, there has been a tendency for status offenders to be "redefined" as criminal offenders so that they still could be processed through the juvenile courts.[17] Almost every status offender does something that can be defined as a criminal event for the purpose of sending the juvenile to an institution.

For example, before the law was changed, a youth who refused to obey his parents could have been brought into court on a charge of incorrigibility, but he would have only been sent to an institution if court officials thought it was in his "best interests." After the law was changed, that youth could not be sent to an institution at all. But if court officials thought it was in the youth's "best interests" to be sent to an institution, then they could charge the youth with some criminal offense. For example, if he threatened a parent or teacher (but did not harm them in any way), he could be charged with simple assault. The youth then could be sent to an institution (since it was in his "best interests"), but would now be labelled a criminal offender rather than a status offender.

The more modest effort to "deinstitutionalize" status offenders has also resulted in redefining status offenders as criminal offenders. This idea was originally embodied in a federal policy that guided the provision of federal funds for juvenile justice to the states. Early figures suggested almost all status offenders were redefined as criminal offenders, so they continued to be institutionalized.[18] Despite this tendency, many judges opposed the policy because they felt they needed the power to institutionalize status offenders directly.[19]

In response to their concerns, federal policy was modified so that a violation of a condition of probation would be considered a criminal offense. Under this modification, a youth charged with a status offense could be brought into court and placed on probation. One of the conditions of probation would be that the youth not commit the status offense again. Youths who committed additional status offenses would be considered to have violated their probation, which would be defined as a criminal offense. These youths then could be sent to an institution.

To some extent, these changes have made the institutionalization of status offenders "invisible."[20] Kids are still institutionalized for truancy, but they are no longer defined as status offenders. They either are charged with some minor criminal offense and institutionalized for that, or school attendance is made a condition of probation so that further truancy is defined as a criminal offense.

It might seem to be a good idea to remove jurisdiction for status offenses from the juvenile court, but the lessons of history suggest that this will never occur—there have been separate laws for juveniles for as far back as history records.

Mitigation of Punishments for Juveniles

A third aspect that has stayed the same for at least two hundred years (and indeed over history) is that juveniles are treated more leniently than adults when they commit the same offenses. That is, when a juvenile is convicted of a crime, the punishment is not as severe as when an adult is convicted of the same crime.

Mitigation in Earlier Times

The Code of Hammurabi, written over 4,000 years ago, indicated that juveniles were to be treated more leniently than adults. In ancient Jewish law, the Talmud specified the conditions under which immaturity was to be considered for more lenient punishment. Under these provisions, there was no corporal punishment before the age of puberty, which was set at 12 for females and 13 for males, and no capital punishment before the age of 20. Similar leniency was found among the Moslems, where children under the age of 17 were generally exempt from retaliation and the death penalty, although they could be corrected.

Roman law also included a lengthy history of mitigated punishments for children. As early as the Twelve Tables (about 450 B.C.), there was absolute immunity from punishment for children below a certain age. Originally, immunity applied only to children who were incapable of speech, but eventually it was applied to all children below the age of 7. In addition, children below puberty have been given reduced punishment under Roman Law since around the year 500 A.D. Justinian, for example, established puberty at 14 for boys and 12 for girls. In between age 7 and puberty, criminal responsibility was made dependent on age, nature of offense, and mental capacity.

Under ancient Saxon law, a child below the age of 12 could not be found guilty of any felony, and a child between 12 and 14 might be acquitted or convicted on the basis of natural capacity. After 14 there was no mitigation.

English common law had acquired its modern form by about the middle of the 1300s, and was summarized by Blackstone in 1769.[21] In general, the law at that time was based on the following framework for mitigating punishments:

Below the age of seven, juveniles have no reponsibility for their actions and therefore cannot be punished for any crimes they commit.

From seven to 14, juveniles are presumed to lack responsibility for their actions, but the prosecution can argue that they should be punished in spite of their youth.

From 14 to 21, juveniles are presumed to be responsible for their actions, but the defense can argue that they should not be punished, despite their age.

After the age of 21, everyone is responsible for their actions and therefore is punished to the full extent of the law.

Mitigation in the Juvenile Court

Today, the juvenile court embodies the concept of less responsibility, and therefore less punishment, for juveniles. In most states, juveniles below the age of 18 are sent to juvenile court when they commit offenses, and the punishments given there are generally more lenient than those in adult courts for similar offenses. A few states have higher or lower ages of juvenile court jurisdiction. For example, in New York State, only juveniles 15 and younger are sent to juvenile court, while those who are 16 and older are tried in adult court.

Juveniles normally sent to juvenile court may be tried instead in adult courts when they commit serious or frequent offenses. Such a procedure goes by a variety of names, including waiver, transfer, certification, and direct filing.[22] Under these provisions, juveniles are treated the same way that youths aged 7 to 14 were treated under English common law: it is presumed that they are not fully responsible for their actions, but the prosecutor can argue that there are special reasons in this case why they should be tried in adult court. If the judge agrees, then the youth is sent to adult court for the full punishment that any adult would receive.

In addition, in some states, certain offenses are not within the jurisdiction of the juvenile court at all, no matter what the child's age. For example, in Pennsylvania, jurisdiction for all homicides lies in criminal courts. Youths charged with homicide are taken directly to criminal court, regardless of how young they are. There, the defense lawyer can argue that, because of immaturity, the youth should be handled in juvenile court. If the judge agrees, the youth can be transferred. These youths are treated the way youths aged 14 to 21 were treated under English Common Law: that is, they are presumed responsible for their actions but the defense may attempt to prove otherwise.

Mitigation as an Aspect That Stays the Same

The specific rules for mitigating punishments for juveniles have changed throughout history. At some times and places, mitigation extends all the way to age 21, while at others only to age 12 or 14. At some times and places, punishments for juveniles are greatly reduced or even eliminated, and at others they are only slightly reduced.

In the future, we can expect that the specific rules for mitigating punishments of juveniles will continue to change, but the mitigation of punishments itself will remain. Whether we provide greater reductions in punishments or lesser, to more juveniles or to fewer, mitigation of punishments will remain a feature of any system for processing juvenile offenders.

Views of Adults about the Behavior of Youth

According to Donovan, "every generation since the dawn of time has denounced the rising generation as being inferior in terms of manners and morals, ethics and honesty."[23] The view that adults have of juveniles is separate from how juveniles actually behave. This view goes as far back as history records, so it probably will remain the same into the future.

Many adults today complain about how rotten kids are, but this was true in Colonial America as well. Harvey Green says:

> One of the most consistent and common themes in the history of relations between American parents and their children is criticism of the younger generation. From almost the moment the settlers of Jamestown and Plymouth stepped off their boats in the early seventeenth century, there arose the cry that children were disobeying their parents as never before.[24]

This phenomenon is not confined to America. Over two thousand years before the Pilgrims, Socrates had his own complaints about youth:

> Children now love luxury. They have bad manners, contempt for authority, they show disrespect for elders and love chatter in place of exercise. They no longer rise when their elders enter the room. They contradict their parents, chatter before company, gobble up dainties at the table, and tyrannize over their teachers.[25]

We can go back even further than that. Fourteen hundred years before Socrates, a Summarian father wrote to his son:

> Because my heart had been sated with weariness of you, I kept away from you and heeded not your fears and grumblings. Because of your clamorings, I was angry with you. Because you do not look to humanity, my heart was carried off as if by an evil wind. Your grumblings have put an end to me; you have brought me to the point of death. . . . Others like you support their parents by working. . . . They multiply barley for their father, maintain him in barley, oil, and wool. You're a man when it comes to perverseness, but compared to them you are not a man at all. You certainly don't labor like them—they are the sons of fathers who make their sons labor, but me, I didn't make you work like them.[26]

Juveniles as Serious Criminals

Most of the above quotes apply to what we now call status offenses. Perhaps kids today are engaged in serious, horrifying crimes, terrible offenses. Today, you might argue, many kids are the worst kind of criminals. There may have been a lot of minor delinquencies in the past, but the serious, hard-core juvenile crime of today is new.

For example, in 1989, *Time* Magazine described "the beast that has broken loose in some of America's young people."[27] The following series of quotations gives a sense of the article while omitting numerous examples presented to illustrate each point:

> More and more teenagers, acting individually or in gangs, are running amuck. . . . To be sure, teenagers have never been angels. Adolescence is often a troubled time of rebellion and rage. . . . But juvenile crime appears to be more widespread and vicious than ever before. . . . Adolescents have always been violence prone, but there are horrendous crimes being committed by even younger children. . . . The teen crime wave flows across all races, classes, and life-styles. The offenders are overwhelmingly male, but girls too are capable of vicious crimes. . . . What is chilling about many of the young criminals is that they show no remorse or conscience, at least initially. Youths brag about their exploits and shrug off victims' pain.

The author suggested that this recent "upsurge in the most violent types of crimes by teens" began in 1983.

However, five years before this juvenile crime wave apparently began, *Time* Magazine seemed to be just as alarmed about the juvenile crime problem:

> Across the U.S., a pattern of crime has emerged that is both perplexing and appalling. Many youngsters appear to be robbing and raping, maiming and murdering as casually as they go to a movie or join a pickup baseball game. A new, remorseless, mutant juvenile seems to have been born, and there is no more terrifying figure in America today.[28]

The author of the 1989 article must have neglected to read this 1978 article. How could the wave of juvenile violence start in 1983 if *Time* had already carried an article about it in 1978?

Views of Adults in Earlier Times

These quotations from *Time* Magazine occur during a time in which juvenile crime, including serious violent and property crime, declined by about one-third. Similar quotations can be found during times when juvenile crime is rising. For example, in 1964, the long-time head of the FBI J. Edgar Hoover was similarly convinced that things had changed:

In the Twenties and Thirties, juvenile delinquency, in general, meant such things as truancy, minor vandalism and petty theft. Today, the term includes armed robbery, assault and even murder. . . . We should not permit actual crimes to be thought of in terms of the delinquencies of a past era. I am not speaking of the relatively minor misdemeanors usually associated with the process of growing up. It is the killings, the rapes and robberies of innocent people by youthful criminals that concern me.[29]

Ten years earlier, in 1954, a New York City judge made a similar statement in *Newsweek,* except that he described the low juvenile crime as being in the 1900s and 1910s, rather than in the 1920s and 1930s:

Back before the first world war, it was a rare day when you saw a man under 25 up for a felony. Today it's the rule. And today when one of these kids robs a bank he doesn't rush for a businesslike getaway. He stays around and shoots up a couple of clerks. Not long ago I asked such a boy why, and he said: "I get a kick out of it when I see blood running."[30]

The article was entitled: "Our Vicious Young Hoodlums: Is There Any Hope?"

That same year, *Time* Magazine ran an article about the "teenage reign of terror (that) has transformed New York City's public school system into a vast incubator of crime in which wayward and delinquent youngsters receive years of 'protection' while developing into toughened and experienced criminals."[31] It said that in some schools, half the pupils carried switchblades or zipguns, others carried homemade flame throwers or plastic water pistols filled with blinding chemical solutions, and other students threatened or beat up teachers who gave them poor grades. It suggested that this behavior had begun "in the past few years."

Views of Adults as an Aspect That Stays the Same

Similar alarms were raised in the 1940s, 1930s, and 1920s.[32] At those times, people believed (as they do today) that the country was being overwhelmed in a rising tide of juvenile delinquency and crime, and that it had not been a serious problem only forty or fifty years ago. Juvenile crime itself seems to go up and down, but the quotations about how terrible juveniles are seem to stay the same. Whether juvenile crime is high or low, many people believe that it is worse today than ever before.

Belief That Juvenile Justice Policy Increases Crime

A fifth aspect of juvenile delinquency and juvenile justice that has stayed
the same for at least two hundred years is a belief that the system for
processing juvenile offenders increases juvenile crime. This belief seems
to be widely held at all times and all places, whether a lot of delinquency
or only a little occurs, and whether juveniles are harshly punished or
leniently treated.

Presently, widespread concern exists that lenient treatment increases
juvenile crime. But that concern tends to alternate in history with the
opposite concern: that harsh punishment increases juvenile crime. Let us
look at these two concerns historically.

Concern That Leniency Increases Juvenile Crime

People have always been concerned that lenient treatment increases
crime among juveniles. This was a major point in the 1978 *Time*
Magazine article quoted above:

> When [a juvenile offender] is caught, the courts usually spew him out again. If
> he is under a certain age, 16 to 18 depending on the state, he is almost always
> taken to juvenile court, where he is treated as if he were still the child he is
> supposed to be. Even if he has murdered someone, he may be put away for
> only a few months. He is either sent home well before his term expires or he
> escapes, which, as the kids say, is "no big deal." Small wonder that hardened
> juveniles laugh, scratch, yawn, mug and even fall asleep while their crimes
> are revealed in court.[33]

Several years earlier, Ted Morgan argued a similar point in an article
entitled "They Think, 'I Can Kill Because I'm 14'."[34] Ten years before
that, J. Edgar Hoover similarly warned against the "misguided policies
which encourage criminal activity, resulting in the arrogant attitude:
"You can't touch me. I'm a juvenile!"[35]

Concern about Leniency in Earlier Times

Today, many people believe that leniency causes juvenile crime and
blame the juvenile justice system for this leniency. They suggest that if
juveniles were tried in adult courts and sent to adult institutions, the
problem would be solved. But the juvenile justice system was originally
established because the adult courts were believed to be too lenient on

juveniles. This suggests that sending juveniles to the adult system will not necessarily result in harsher treatment.

This story will be discussed in more detail in Chapter 5, but I will make the basic point here. Before the establishment of the first juvenile institution in New York City in 1825, only adult prisons were available for punishing juveniles. These were viewed as very harsh places that would increase the likelihood that juveniles would commit more crime. Prosecutors, judges, and juries in the criminal courts all naturally tried to avoid sending juvenile offenders to these institutions, with the result that many were freed with no punishment at all.[36]

The chief judge in New York was concerned that freeing these juveniles without any punishment encouraged them to commit further crime. He helped establish the first juvenile institution to receive these youngsters who otherwise would get off scot-free. One year after the establishment of the institution, the New York City District Attorney stated that the new institution had solved the problem.[37]

Around that same time, a "Report of the Committee for Investigating the Causes of the Alarming Increase of Juvenile Delinquency in the Metropolis" was issued in London that expressed similar concerns.[38] The problem, as it existed in both London and New York, was that only harsh punishments were available in the adult system, but that the natural tendency to provide more lenient treatments to juveniles resulted in many of them being let off without any punishment whatsoever. The juvenile justice system was originally invented to correct this problem: its goal was to provide some punishments for those who were receiving no punishments at all from the adult system.

Concern about Harshness Increasing Crime

Just as there have been concerns for a long time that leniency increases juvenile crime, there also have been concerns that harsh punishments increase juvenile crime. For example, many law-abiding adults committed at least some crimes when they were juveniles for which they might have been sent to an institution. Most of them were not caught or, if caught, received lenient treatment. Most of them then quit committing crimes, since their behavior was part of growing up.

Now suppose instead of this lenient treatment, they had been sent to an institution. Such harsh punishment might have increased the likelihood that they would continue to commit crimes in the future, rather than simply growing out of it. This is the purpose of leniency—to allow juveniles to "get out while the getting is good."

Concern about Harshness in Earlier Times

This has not just been a concern in recent times. For example, the judge in New York City in the early 1820s was quoted above as being concerned that letting juveniles off scot-free would encourage them to commit crime. That same judge was also concerned that sending juveniles to the prisons and jails would be "a fruitful source of pauperism, a nursery of new vices and crimes, a college for the perfection of adepts in guilt."[39] That is, this judge had to choose between providing harsh punishments or doing nothing at all, and he believed that both choices increased crime among juveniles.

A similar concern about harshness later provided the motivation for establishing the first juvenile court in Chicago in 1899 (see Chapter 6). Because of an Illinois Supreme Court decision in 1870, lenient handling of juvenile offenders was severely restricted. This meant that juvenile justice officials faced the same dilemma as the earlier officials in New York City: they either had to provide harsh punishments to juvenile offenders or they could do nothing at all. Like the New York City judge, they believed that both choices increased crime among juveniles. The juvenile court was invented partly to provide lenient treatments for juveniles who were being harshly punished in Chicago's jails and poorhouses, and partly to provide lenient treatments for juveniles for whom nothing was being done at all in the adult courts.

Concern about Juvenile Justice Policy Stays the Same

If you think about the problem faced by officials in New York and London in the early 1800s and in Chicago in the late 1800s, then it becomes apparent that the concern that leniency causes juvenile crime and that harshness causes juvenile crime are really two sides of the same coin. Their relation is described by what Walker calls the "law of criminal justice thermodynamics":

> An increase in the severity of the penalty will result in less frequent application of the penalty.[40]

This "law" explains the basic problem faced by these officials.[41] Only harsh punishments were available to respond to juvenile crime. Some juveniles received those punishments, but others were let off because the punishments seemed inappropriate and counterproductive. In terms of the above "law," the penalties were so severe that they were infrequently applied.

Another way to phrase it is to say that *certainty and severity are enemies.* If you increase the severity of a penalty, you usually decrease the certainty with which it is applied. If you want to increase the certainty with which a penalty is applied, usually you must reduce its severity. This is exactly what criminal justice officials in London, New York, and Chicago did: they reduced the severity of penalties for juveniles in order to increase the certainty of applying them. That is, they established a "lenient" juvenile justice system.

The continual concern about the effectiveness of juvenile justice policies arises from this relationship between certainty and severity. If juvenile justice policies provide harsh punishments, then some juveniles will receive those punishments but others will receive no punishment at all because the punishments seem inappropriate and counterproductive. Concern about the effectiveness of these policies arises because both of these two choices are thought to increase crime.

But if the policies provide lenient treatments, then many juveniles receive the treatments but some laugh and feel free to commit serious crime with impunity. Concern about the effectiveness of these policies arises because people believe that if we had only "gotten tough" with these juveniles earlier, then the serious crimes would never have occurred.

The Cycle of Juvenile Justice

Juvenile offenders always are treated more leniently than adults who commit the same offenses, and juveniles who initially commit minor offenses are treated very leniently by the justice system. At least some of these juveniles go on to commit serious crimes. Many people conclude that these serious crimes would not have occurred if the juvenile had been punished severely for the earlier offenses. They argue that leniency encourages juveniles to laugh at the system, to believe they will not be punished no matter what they do, and to feel free to commit more frequent and serious crimes.

In response to these views, justice officials begin to "toughen up" their responses to juvenile offenders, and the "lenient" responses become less available. Some minor offenders receive the harsh punishments, but others are released because the harsh punishments seem ineffective and counterproductive.

Despite "getting tough," juvenile crime rates remain high (as they always do). Some minor offenders who received harsh punishments go on to commit serious crimes, along with some of those who were let off. This generates increased efforts to provide even harsher punishments. But as the penalties become more severe, they are less frequently applied: even more minor offenders are released with no punishment at all. The juvenile crime rate still remains high.

Throughout all of this, many people remain convinced that the "juvenile crime wave" began only recently, that it did not exist back in the "good old days," and that it can be ended through proper justice policies. Eventually, enough time passes so that the "good old days" was before the whole "get tough" movement began, when juvenile offenders were treated leniently.

Since they are now convinced that there was no problem of serious juvenile crime back then, they conclude that harsh punishments actually increase juvenile crime. Like the reformers in New York and London in the early 1800s and in Chicago in the late 1800s, they argue that these punishments embitter the juveniles, cut off their legitimate options, and teach them the ways of crime. They also argue that harsh punishments indirectly increase juvenile crime because so many juveniles are let off scot-free when only harsh punishments are available.

The juvenile system then is reformed to take account of this argument, and juvenile offenders once again receive lenient punishments. But juvenile crime rates remain high, adults remain convinced that the problem is recent and that it did not exist in the "good old days," and that it can be solved through proper justice policies. Eventually, enough time passes so that the "good old days" are back when officials "got tough" with juvenile offenders. Because people are now convinced that there was no problem with serious juvenile crime back then, they naturally conclude that the problem lies in the leniency with which juvenile offenders are now treated. A new reform movement then reintroduces harsh punishments.

The "cycle of juvenile justice" arises from the fact that juvenile crime rates remain high, regardless of justice policies that are in effect at the time. But many people are always convinced that these high rates only occurred recently, that back in the "good old days" juvenile crime was low, and that juvenile crime would be low again if only we had the proper justice policies in effect. These people then generate continual pressure to abandon whatever justice policies are in effect at the time and replace them with new policies. Because only a limited number of policies are possible to begin with, the result is that the juvenile justice system tends to cycle back and forth between harshness and leniency.

This cycle cannot be broken by any particular juvenile justice policy since every conceivable policy confronts the same dilemma: after it is implemented, many people will continue to be convinced that juvenile crime is exceptionally high, that it was not a serious problem in the "good old days," and that it would not be a serious problem today if we only had the proper justice policies in effect.

This dilemma confronts not only our current juvenile justice system but also any conceivable organizational arrangement for processing juvenile offenders. Earlier organizational arrangements for processing juvenile offenders grappled with (and were discarded because of) the same dilemma. New and different organizational arrangements that might be created in the future to process juvenile offenders would soon confront the same dilemma.

Notes

1. Travis Hirschi and Michael Gottfredson, "Age and the explanation of crime," *American Journal of Sociology*, 89:552–84 (1983). See also Frank R. Donovan, *Wild Kids*, Stackpole, Harrisburg, 1967 and Wiley B. Sanders, ed., *Juvenile Offenders for a Thousand Years*, University of North Carolina Press, Chapel Hill, 1970.

2. Paul Strasburg, *Violent Juvenile Offenders: An Anthology*, NCCD, San Francisco, 1984.

3. Negley K. Teeters and David Matza, "The Extent of Delinquency in the United States," pp. 2–15 in Ruth Shonle Cavan, ed., *Readings in Juvenile Delinquency*, Lippincott, Philadelphia, 1964; Sophia M. Robison, *Juvenile Delinquency*, Holt, Rinehart and Winston, New York, 1960, Chapter 2; Walter C. Reckless and Mapheus Smith, *Juvenile Delinquency*, McGraw-Hill, New York, 1932, Chapter 2.

4. Clyde B. Vedder, *The Juvenile Offender*, Doubleday, Garden City, NY, 1954, p. 26.

5. The year 1952 was the first one in which the tables were labelled as representing arrests in cities with 2,500 or more population. This raises the possibility that some of the rise in the proportion of juvenile arrests might result from changes in data collection. See Teeters and Matza, op, cit.

6. Philip J. Cook and John H. Laub, "Trends in Child Abuse and Juvenile Delinquency," in Francis X. Hartmann, ed., *From Children to Citizens: The Role of the Juvenile Court*, Springer-Verlag, New York, 1987.

7. Hibbert, op. cit., p. 433.

8. Quoted in Teeters and Matza, op. cit., p. 4.

9. James Gilbert, *A Cycle of Outrage*, Oxford, New York, 1986, pp. 24–26.

10. James A. Inciardi, Alan A. Block, and Lyle A. Hallowell, *Historical Approaches to Crime*, Sage, Beverly Hills, 1977, pp. 59–89.

11. These articles are described in Archer Butler Hulbert, "The Habit of Going to the Devil," *Atlantic Monthly* 138:804–6 (December, 1926). See Teeters and Matza, op. cit.

12. Sanders, op. cit., p. 135.

13. Hibbert, op. cit., p. 432.

14. E.g., see Curt R. Bartol and Anne M. Bartol, *Juvenile Delinqency*, Prentice-Hall, Englewood Cliffs, 1989. For a review of theories of crime generally, see George B. Vold and Thomas J. Bernard, *Theoretical Criminology*, Oxford, New York, 1986.

15. Exodus 21:15; Leviticus 20:9.

16. John R. Sutton, *Stubborn Children*, University of California Press, Berkeley, 1988, p. 11. See also Lee E. Teitelbaum and Leslie J. Harris, "Some Historical Perspectives on Governmental Regulation of Children and Parents," in Teitelbaum and Aiden R. Gough, eds., *Beyond Control: Status Offenders in the Juvenile Court*, Ballinger, Cambridge, MA, 1977, pp. 1–44.

17. Thomas C. Castellano, "The Justice Model in the Juvenile Justice System: Washington State's Experience," *Law & Policy* 8(4):479–506 (October, 1986).

18. Ira M. Schwartz, *(In)justice for Juveniles*, D. C. Heath, Lexington, 1989, pp. 2–3.

19. Gordon A. Raley and John E. Dean, "The Juvenile Justice and Delinquency Prevention Act: Federal Leadership in State Reform," *Law & Policy* 8(4):397–418 (October, 1986).

20. Frederic L. Faust and Paul J. Brantingham, *Juvenile Justice Philosophy*, West, St. Paul, 1979, p. 460.

21. Sir William Blackstone, *Commentaries on the Laws of England*, IV, London, 1795, p. 23.

22. See H. Ted Rubin, *Juvenile Justice*, Random House, New York, 1985, Chapter 2.

23. Donovan, op. cit., p. 11.

24. Harvey Green, "Scientific Thought and the Nature of Children in America, 1820–1920," in *A Century of Childhood, 1820–1920*, Strong Museum, Rochester, NY, 1984, p. 121.

25. Quoted in Gary F. Jensen and Dean G. Rojek, *Delinquency*. Heath, Lexington, 1980, p. 2.

26. Samuel Noah Dramer, "A Father and His Perverse Son," *Crime and Delinquency* 3(2):169–73 (April, 1957).

27. Anastasia Toufexis, "Our Violent Kids," *Time Magazine*, June 12, 1989, pp. 52–58. See also the editorial "Meltdown in our Cities," in *U.S. News and World Report*, May 29, 1989, for similar arguments.

28. "The Youth Crime Plague," *Time Magazine* July 11, 1977, pp. 18–28.

29. Hoover, op. cit. For a similar article written one year earlier, see Judith Viorst, "Delinquency! National Crisis," *Science News Letter*, 84:202–3 (September 28, 1963).

30. "Our Vicious Young Hoodlums: Is There Any Hope?" *Newsweek Magazine* 44:43–44 (September 6, 1954).

31. "The New Three Rs," *Time Magazine* 63(6):68–70 (March 15, 1954). This is based on a special series appearing in the New York *Daily News* the preceding week.

32. E.g., J. Edgar Hoover, "The Crime Wave We Now Face," *The New York Times Magazine*, April 21, 1946, pp. 26–27; "Children Without Morals," *Time Magazine* 40:24 (October 5, 1942); Leonard V. Harrison and Pryor M. Grant, *Youth in the Toils*, Macmillan, New York, 1939; Clyde A. Tolson, "Youth and Crime," *Vital Speeches* 2:468–72 (April 20, 1936); and "Youth Leads the Criminal Parade," *The Literary Digest*, 113:20 (April 23, 1932). For alarms raised in even earlier times, see Hulbert, op. cit.

33. "Youth Crime Plague," op. cit.

34. *New York Times* Magazine, January 19, 1975. A similar article appeared in the same magazine thirteen years earlier, but with an emphasis on the social causes of delinquency rather than on lenient treatment. See Ira Henry Freeman, "The Making of a Boy Killer," *New York Times* Magazine, February 18, 1962, pp. 14ff.

35. Hoover, op. cit., p. 668.

36. Robert M. Mennel, *Thorns and Thistles*, University Press of New England, Hanover, NH, 1973, pp. xxv–xxvi.

37. Bradford Kinney Peirce, *A Half Century with Juvenile Delinquents*, Patterson-Smith, Montclair, 1969, p. 79.

38. Sanders, op. cit., p. 111.

39. Quoted in Peirce, op. cit., pp. 41–42.

40. Samuel Walker, *Sense and Nonsense About Crime*, 2nd ed., Brooks/Cole, Pacific Grove, 1989, pp. 46–48.

41. We face similar problems today. For example, homicide is punished more severely than any other crime. Franklin Zimring, Sheila O'Malley, and Joel Eigen ("Punishing Homicide in Philadelphia," *University of Chicago Law Review* 43:252, Winter, 1976) found that homicide defendants who did not receive a very severe punishment typically received little or no punishment at all. They concluded: "The problem is not that our system is too lenient or too severe; sadly, it is both." At the other end of the scale, minor delinquencies are punished the most leniently, and often result in diversion from the juvenile justice system. The problem here has been that, because the punishments are so lenient, they have tended to be very broadly applied. The phrase used to describe this is "widening the net"—i.e., diversion programs are compared to a fishing boat dragging an ever-widening net that sweeps up more and more fish. See James Austin and Barry Krisberg, "Wider, Stronger, and Different Nets," *Journal of Research in Crime and Delinquency* 18:165–96 (1981).

4

The Origin of Juvenile Delinquency

The term "juvenile delinquency" was invented almost two hundred years ago. One of its first uses was in a "Report of the Committee for Investigating the Causes of the Alarming Increase of Juvenile Delinquency in the Metropolis," which came out in London in 1816.[1] This was soon followed by the founding of a "Society for the Reformation of Juvenile Delinquents" in New York City in 1819,[2] and the new term spread rapidly. Prior to that time, children who committed offenses were described as "black-guard children," "stubborn children," "poor vagrant children," or they were simply labelled young criminals.

The modern juvenile justice system originated about the same time that the term was invented, with the establishment of the first juvenile institution in New York City in 1825. The first juvenile court was established seventy-five years later in Chicago in 1899. Before then, juveniles who committed offenses were tried in the same courts and received the same punishments as adults. The only difference was that juveniles usually received less punishment than adults who committed the same offense. The origin of the juvenile justice system is presented in Chapters 5 and 6.

This chapter argues that juvenile delinquency itself originated about the same time as the term "juvenile delinquency" and as the juvenile justice system. This is a surprising argument, especially for those who believe that juvenile delinquency remains the same throughout history. It suggests that there really were "good old days" two hundred years ago when there was no juvenile delinquency in the sense that we mean it today.

There are two meanings to the statement that juvenile delinquency originated around the year 1800. The first refers to delinquency as a modern phenomenon. There is a sense in which the behaviors we describe as juvenile delinquency first appeared around the year 1800 and simply did not exist before. The second meaning refers to delinquency as a modern idea. The term "juvenile delinquency" reflects a particular way of understanding and interpreting youthful offending, where that way of thinking originated around the year 1800.

Juvenile Delinquency as a Modern Phenomenon

Juvenile delinquency appears as a modern phenomenon when traditional (i.e., rural and agricultural) societies make the transition to modern (i.e., urban and industrial) societies. The United States and Western Europe made this transition between the years 1760 and 1840, so that was when the problem of juvenile delinquency first appeared. More recently, Eastern European societies made the same transition, and even more recently the developing nations of Asia, Africa, and Latin America. As each country underwent modernization, it was confronted with a new "problem of juvenile delinquency" that it did not have when it was a traditional (rural and agricultural) society.[3]

Five different factors can be involved in the development of this phenomenon, although all are not necessarily involved every time it appears. *Traditional mechanisms* for responding to juvenile offending break down as part of the breakdown of the traditional society, which can increase the volume of juvenile offending. *Urbanization* brings juvenile offenders into close contact with each other and with potential victims, both of which add to the tendency of juveniles to commit offenses. *Industrialization* increases the number of moveable goods and leads to a rise in property crime, much of which is committed by juveniles. Industrialization often is accompanied by a sudden *population growth*, which increases the proportion of young people in the population. Since crime is disproportionately committed by young males, this leads to an increase in the total volume of crime. Finally, societies establish *modern juvenile justice systems,* which detect and process juvenile offenders more efficiently, which results in higher official statistics on juvenile crime. These systems can also generate juvenile crime by institutionalizing juveniles who would have remained in the community in earlier times.

The Breakdown of Traditional Mechanisms

Prior to 1760 in America, neither crime in general nor juvenile crime in particular was a serious problem. For example, Ferdinand said that in Massachusetts

> neither adults nor adolescents committed many crimes before the Revolution (in 1776), and more often than not those few adolescents who were charged with criminal offenses escaped severe punishment by a general unwillingness of juries to convict them. Most of the crimes by adolescents were handled informally in the community by denunciations in church or at town meetings and usually followed by public confessions and pleas for forgiveness. There was no concept of adolescence or juvenile delinquency, and though the crimes of young people were typically less violent than those committed by adults, they were otherwise very similar.[4]

There were no special institutions or facilities for dealing with youthful offenders, so that parents were simply required by law and custom to control their own children.[5]

This was the major mechanism for controlling delinquency in traditional societies, and it worked well in the small towns and rural areas before 1700. After about 1700, however, increasing dissatisfaction with the performance of parents in this traditional task arose. This resulted in an increasing number of shrill laws threatening parents who failed in this duty.[6]

For children who could not be controlled by their own families, the second traditional mechanism was to bind them out to other families assumed better at accomplishing this task. These youths usually were required to work as servants to earn their keep.[7]

This second mechanism for controlling delinquency in traditional societies also began breaking down during the 1700s for several reasons.

The families who took these children were increasingly dissatisfied with them, since older and more difficult children were being brought into the system and these children frequently deserted before having served their time.[8] In addition, a wider availability of slaves and other indentured servants existed who could fill these roles.[9]

Corporal and capital punishments were a third means of control, and had been used with many juvenile offenders. But by 1800 or so, these punishments were becoming very unpopular, and juveniles were exempted from some corporal punishments by law in some states. Transportation (e.g., from England to America or Australia) was briefly used as a fourth mechanism after the decline of corporal punishments, but soon no other place would accept the criminals being transported.

Thus, all the traditional methods for responding to youthful offenders had broken down by the end of the 1700s. Youthful offenders therefore were boarded out at public expense or housed in the newly founded adult prisons for long periods.[10] These were unpopular options, generally seen as expensive and even counterproductive. Consequently, juries often refused to convict juveniles, preferring to release them with no punishment whatsoever.[11]

Industrialization

Before industrialization, there was a lower total volume of crime and most were violent crimes such as murder, rape, and assault.[12] After industrialization, there was a higher total volume of crime and most were property crimes such as burglary, robbery, and larceny-theft. This change was a direct result of industrialization itself, which mass produces moveable goods that can be stolen.

Before industrialization, most of what people owned was not very moveable, so there was very little stealing. For example, until around the year 1300, land was the primary form of wealth, and this could not really be stolen in a modern sense.[13] By about 1500, however, wealth could be accumulated in the form of moveable goods that were either traded for other goods or sold for money. Only at this point could stealing become a real problem.

In England, this led to the famous "carrier's case" in 1473, in which the law of theft took on its modern form.[14] The defendant in the case was hired by a merchant to carry some bales to Southampton, but instead took the bales himself. According to the law of the time, this was not a theft because the merchant had freely given the bales to the carrier. It required an imaginative ruling by the judge to conclude that a theft had taken place. The point is that, as late as 1473, the law of theft in England was very simple because theft was not much of a problem.

Today, about 90% of all crimes are property crimes, such as burglary, larceny, and auto theft. The likelihood that something will be stolen is directly affected by how moveable it is. In 1975, for example, $26.44 in motor vehicles and parts were stolen for every $100 that were legally purchased, as compared with only $0.12 worth of furniture.[15] Thus, in the days before industrialization when most possessions were things like furniture, there was very little stealing.

Juveniles have always committed a larger proportion of property crimes than adults. As property crimes became the most prominent form of crime, juveniles became the most prominent type of criminals. Thus, this new crime wave came to be seen, to some extent, as a juvenile crime wave.[16]

Urbanization

Before the 1800s, European and American societies were largely rural and agricultural. There were some cities, but European societies before the 1800s were overwhelmingly rural.[17] The cities that existed were small, with few having more than 10,000 people. The vast majority of people lived in small villages that could not even be called towns, much less cities. The rural nature of European society persisted into the 1800s.

> As late as 1801, when the Industrial Revolution was still getting under way, the United Kingdom, although it was then the most urbanized nation in the world, had only one city of more than 100,000 inhabitants. This city (London), the largest in Europe and probably in the world, accounted for only 4.7 per cent of the U.K. population.[18]

America was similarly rural and agricultural. In 1760, a large majority of towns in America had fewer than 1,000 people, and only a few places had more than 2,500.[19] The largest city in the country in that year was Philadelphia with 23,750 people. New York City had a population of 18,000 and Boston 15,000, but no other city in America had more than 10,000 people.[20]

Industrialization brought with it a vast expansion in urbanization because it freed people from working on the land and provided them with jobs in factories, which could be located in urban areas. By 1840, Western Europe and America suddenly looked more like our world today—urban and industrial rather than rural and agricultural. Especially in England and Germany, societies suddenly were transformed from almost entirely agricultural to increasingly industrial. By 1841, only about one-third of occupied males in England were employed in agriculture, forestry, and fishing.[21] Before 1800, England had only one city of more than 100,000 people, but by 1851 it had twelve such cities.[22] London's population rose to 2.25 million by 1845.[23] Other cities also experienced explosive growth. For example, in the fifty-seven years between 1774 and 1831, Manchester's population grew from 29,000 to 228,000.[24]

A similar phenomenon occurred in America. In 1820, for example, the population of New York City was about 120,000 and was growing rapidly in response to immigration.[25] It was becoming a modern city: densely inhabited and increasingly chaotic, with many different racial and ethnic groups. Boston in 1850 had grown to 137,000.[26]

In making the transition to city life, many families simply disintegrated, and homeless children and adolescents began to congregate in groups on the streets of the rapidly growing cities.[27] Many took up stealing as a means of survival since the urban environment brought them into close contact both with likely victims who had moveable goods that could be stolen and with other youths like themselves whom they could cooperate with in stealing ventures. In addition, the urban environment offered these youths few other realistic courses of action for their survival.

These children and youths were a new and serious problem, one that did not exist in the "good old days" before urbanization and industrialization. Thus, they were described by a new term: "juvenile delinquents."

Youth Population and the Juvenile Justice System

Two additional factors may have played a role in the new problem of juvenile delinquency. First, the size of the crime problem usually is closely linked to the relative proportion of young males in the population, since this group commits more crime than others.[28] A population boom in

England during the beginning of the 1800s resulted in a large proportion of young males in London, and may have contributed to the perception that there was a "juvenile crime wave."

No comparable youth explosion was apparent in the United States until the middle of that century, when there was a very large rise in violent crime.[29] However, a large rise in the *rate* of juvenile delinquency occurred in Boston after about 1840 (i.e., holding the youth population constant), as well as in the *seriousness* of the offenses that delinquents committed.[30] After examining a number of possible explanations, Ferdinand concluded that these changes were *caused by* the new juvenile justice system that locked up minor and status offenders in institutions to prevent them from going on to becoming serious property offenders. In fact, it appears that this policy drove these minor offenders into more frequent and serious offenses.

Juvenile Delinquents as Potential Property Offenders

Juvenile delinquency as a modern phenomenon emerged in Western Europe and America around the year 1800 because that is when those societies underwent the processes of urbanization and industrialization. Urban property crime by lower-class persons then became the major type of crime in the whole society. Young people committed more than their share of this crime and this new type of crime was subsequently described as "juvenile delinquency." Thus, "juvenile delinquents" originally were lower-class juveniles who stole property from middle- and upper-class adults in urban settings.

Urban property crime by poor young people is the basic problem that was defined as juvenile delinquency, but a major emphasis of the emerging juvenile justice policies was on children and youths who might commit these crimes *in the future*. Poor, vagrant youths who were congregating in groups in the cities had few options besides stealing for surviving. Thus, the founders of the juvenile justice system were not especially concerned with whether these youths had actually committed these offenses yet. The emphasis became on getting them off the streets on the assumption that they would commit these offenses soon enough, if they had not yet actually done so.

Juvenile Delinquency as a Modern Idea

In addition to this new phenomenon of juvenile delinquency, a new way of understanding and interpreting offending behavior by juveniles also arose. This new idea was used to understand the new form of crime that just had appeared on the scene, but it was also used for all other offending behaviors by juveniles that had been around since the dawn of time.

The new idea was that juveniles were vulnerable to the influences of other people, whether good or bad. They were "malleable" like clay—they could be shaped and molded and formed into whatever was wanted. Once they grew up, however, they "set" just like clay that was baked in the oven. The shape became permanent and, whether good or bad, it could no longer be changed.

The "old" idea was that people were largely unchangeable—they were what they were and nothing could be done about it. The new idea was that, while adults were indeed unchangeable, children were not yet "fixed" into a set pattern. They could be influenced toward the good, if one got to them early enough. The implication was that the good people, the law-abiding citizens, should intervene early and aggressively in the lives of youth who were in danger of being shaped and molded and formed into criminals. These children could be rescued rather easily while they were still young, but as they grew older they soon could not be saved at all.

The invention of the new term "juvenile delinquent" reflected this new concept that juveniles were malleable. If you look up the word "delinquent" in the dictionary, you will find that it literally refers to someone who has failed to do what is required. For example, a person may be "delinquent" in paying taxes. This term directed attention away from the crimes that the child committed and toward the notion that the child was failing to carry out the obligations of a responsible member of society. Thus, where the term "young criminal" suggested that we respond with punishment, the term "juvenile delinquent" suggested that we respond with efforts to shape and mold and form the youth into a responsible society member.

The Idea of Juvenile

To have an idea of juvenile delinquency, you must have the idea of "juvenile"—that is, you must think about juveniles as a group who are similar to each other and different from other people in at least some ways. You might think that the idea of "juvenile" is something that stays the same in history, that everyone would always have recognized juveniles as a group in this sense, and that therefore this idea has not changed in the past and will not change in the future. But in fact, the idea of juvenile is fairly recent in origin and has varied greatly over time.

Aries[31] presented the first argument about changes in ideas about childhood over the centuries. Specifically, he argued that there were two separate ideas of childhood over the centuries, the first emerging around the year 1400 and the second around the year 1600.

No Idea of Childhood

According to Aries, no idea of childhood at all was present until somewhere around the year 1400. Children existed, of course, but there was a sense in which people did not recognize their existence. Children who were still in the care of women (i.e., below the age of 5 or 6) were treated as if they did not exist at all, and children who were older were treated as if they were people like everyone else. Thus, "children," as a category in people's minds, did not exist.

This might seem like a strange argument, but consider slaves as an example. For the slaveholder, young children who were still in the care of women simply did not count as slaves. It was not that the slaveholder thought they were free—rather, it would be more accurate to say that, in the view of the slaveholder, they did not exist at all. But as soon as those children left the care of women, they became slaves like everyone else. They were not children or adolescent or adult slaves—they were just slaves.

That point is illustrated by the common practice of calling slaves "boy" or "girl," no matter what their age. While it is obvious that slaves aged like everyone else, slaveholders generally did not distinguish among slaves on that basis. That is, the slaveholder had "no idea of childhood" when it came to slaves.

This was the way of understanding or interpreting all people in earlier times—it simply held on longer with slaveholders than with other groups. Before the year 1400 or so, there was a sense in which all people viewed each other in the same way that slaveholders later viewed slaves—they did not see children as "existing" until they were out of the care of women, and after that point they were just "people" like everyone else. There was no idea of childhood despite the obvious fact that children existed.

This view originated because of high fertility and high infant mortality: people had many children, and a great many of them died before the age of 5 or 6. As late as the 1600s, approximately two-thirds of all children died before the age of 4.[32] The combination of high fertility and high infant mortality meant that the mere birth of a baby did not really count. Many babies were born but most would soon die and never grow up to become adults.

To protect themselves from the devastation that would come from the child's death, people largely did not become attached to children until they had passed the point at which death was a likely event. Once the child was 6 or 7 and had a fair chance of living to become an adult, then adults began to treat the child as if he or she were real. Before that, people treated the child as if the child had not yet quite achieved the status of a person. Rather, children were seen as being "in a sort of limbo, hanging between life and death, more as a kind of animal than a human being, without mental activities or recognizable bodily shape."[33]

This way of "seeing" children was not due to ignorance or evil, but to the terrible conditions under which people lived: most of these children would die and there was nothing you could do.[34] Only when children were 5 or 6 would you begin to assume that they would live, so that you could become attached to them. Before that, it was simply too dangerous.

The First Idea of Childhood

Somewhere around the year 1400, the first idea of childhood developed. It arose because infant mortality began to decline. As it became more likely that the child would live, parents began to become more attached to their children at earlier ages.

This first idea viewed the child as a source of pleasure and joy. Imagine a parent tickling and talking to an infant. The parent talks baby-talk, cuddles and plays with the baby, and generally experiences a lot of pleasure and joy in the infant that comes from the love and attachment they feel. According to Aries, the willingness to feel and express this love and attachment originated around the year 1400 in response to declining rates of infant mortality. That is, because the baby was not quite so likely to die, parents allowed themselves to become attached to the infant, but still did not count on that baby's becoming an adult.

This first idea of childhood originated with parents, and while it had many positive aspects, it also had negative ones. Because there still was no clear expectation that the child would grow into an adult, there was no special attempt to shape or form the child. Often the child was simply "used" for pleasure, with half a view that the child would die anyway so it didn't matter.[35]

The Second Idea of Childhood

Around the year 1600, the second idea of childhood developed—the child as a potential adult. This development occurred because of a further decline in the infant mortality rate, and it remains our view of children today. We expect that each infant who is born will grow up to become an adult, and we treat that infant accordingly.

This idea originated with teachers and moralists rather than with parents.[36] They were offended by the abuse and neglect of children that arose out of first idea. But these moralists and teachers added something else: Puritanism was on the rise, and they believed that humans had fallen from grace because of their sin in the Garden of Eden. Therefore, they believed that human nature was fundamentally inclined toward evil. Children, being human, were thought to be inclined toward evil from the very moment of birth.[37]

These moralists were appalled by the behavior of adults in their societies, but the adults seemed to be a lost cause because they were so set in their ways. Children exhibited the same natural inclinations toward evil as adults, but they could still be influenced if proper techniques were used. Children could be shaped and molded and formed into righteous, law-abiding, God-fearing adults.

Thus, the second idea of childhood contained four elements: (1) that the infant was naturally inclined toward evil because of the fallen human nature; (2) that infants will grow up to become adults and become set in their evil ways, when it will be too late to do anything about it; (3) that infants and children were still malleable and could be shaped and molded and formed into a righteous, God-fearing, law-abiding adults; and that (4) in the long run this would result in a righteous, God-fearing, law-abiding society.

Colleges as the First Great Battleground

At the time this idea of childhood emerged, around the year 1600, Western Europe was still mostly organized around feudalism, in which people were tied to the land in a hereditary system of rights and obligations. Some of those people were peasants and others were nobles, but all were locked in an unchanging system that had been in place for hundreds of years.

Within the heart of that feudal system, however, a new system was slowly growing: capitalism. Under capitalism, people are not tied in fixed and unchanging roles. Instead, they are free to sell their labor to the highest bidder or purchase the labor of anyone willing to sell it.

The people who purchased the labor of others (e.g., merchants, bankers, industrialists) increasingly sent their sons to universities, so that they would be educated to take over the family businesses. But up until about the year 1500, universities were pretty loosely organized places. There was no admissions procedure or school calendar—students would just show up and begin to sit in on classes, which were held in rooms rented by the Masters.

There were no dormitories for university students, so they would rent private lodgings, frequently located over a bar and next to a whorehouse. There, they lived totally unsupervised lives. The result was a lot of crime and violence. For example, one contemporary account states: "The students of Paris attacked and slew passersby, carried off the women, ravished the virgins, committed robberies and broke into houses."[38]

The teachers and moralists of the day attempted to get control of this student population by establishing colleges. Colleges originally were boardinghouses for university students with rules and supervision. Parents of the students who, like many parents today, had to pay for the student to attend the classes, would pay extra for the student to live in the colleges. That, at least, gave them some hope that the kid might actually learn something.

At the beginning, there was an all-out war between students and the teachers and moralists who ran these colleges. But, by sometime in the 1700s, the war was largely won, as the social control exerted by the teachers and moralists began to be passed from parent to child. That is, the teachers no longer had to contend with totally unsocialized youth, but rather their socialized parents had already instilled some control in their children.

Thus, the idea that the young should be shaped, molded, formed, and created into the kind of adults you wanted was first applied to the children of the emerging capitalists. It was only later used to become the basis of the juvenile justice system, when it would be applied to the children of the urban poor. This transition would be mediated by the emergence of another idea: adolescence.

The Idea of Adolescence

Where the second idea of childhood had emerged around the year 1600, the idea of adolescence did not emerge until the 1800s.[39] This extended the second idea of childhood into the teenage years and applied it to the children of the working and lower classes rather than the children of capitalists.

In earlier times, these youths simply were viewed as adults—they left their parents' house, worked like everyone else, married, and had children. But this changed with the urbanization and industrialization that began around the year 1800. These lower- and working-class young people increasingly lost their economic independence since they were the last ones hired and the first ones fired in the new industries. They therefore remained at home and dependent on their parents for much longer periods.

At the same time, because they were located in urban areas, they were free to roam about with other youths who were dislocated and unattached. The result was the same for these poor youths as two hundred years earlier with the children of capitalists: a great deal of crime and violence.

At that point, teachers and moralists applied the second idea of childhood to lower- and working-class adolescents. These youths were potential adults, and they had not become set in their ways. They could still be shaped and molded and formed into responsible members of society. This could only be done by intervening while they were still adolescents. Once they became adults, they could no longer be changed and would become set in their ways.

The Idea of Juvenile Delinquency

The new "idea" of juvenile delinquency was formed out of these components: it consisted of the second idea of childhood, extended into the teenage years and redefined as adolescence, applied to the children of the lower and working classes in urban areas, and specifically to their behavior in stealing property from wealthier people. These children and adolescents, the new idea held, could be shaped and molded and formed into God-fearing, law-abiding adults. In particular, they could be stopped from committing property crimes.

The battle to control lower- and working-class adolescents, however, could not take place in the colleges, since they did not attend them. Some new system had to be created that could capture these youths so that they could be shaped, molded, and formed. That new system would be the juvenile justice system.

Juvenile Delinquency as a Phenomenon and an Idea

Today, juvenile offenders often are described as "hardened" criminals. This description means that the original idea of juvenile delinquency has been rejected: "hardened" means they are not malleable, not susceptible to being shaped and molded and formed into law-abiding, God-fearing adults. People who view young offenders in this way usually also reject the term "juvenile delinquent," and tend to use some other term like "young criminal." These same people often reject the juvenile justice system and want young criminals handled in criminal court just like adults.

Thus, while the *phenomenon* of juvenile delinquency is still a part of our modern world, the *idea* of juvenile delinquency is under increasing attack and could be abandoned in the near future. If it were abandoned, then the juvenile justice system probably would be abandoned along with it.

We now turn to the events by which our present juvenile justice system emerged from this philosophical and historical context. The next two chapters focus on two specific times and places: New York City around the year 1825 when the first juvenile institution was founded and Chicago around 1899 when the first juvenile court was established.

These chapters provide specific examples of the general argument made above that juvenile delinquency emerged as a modern phenomenon and as a modern idea interpreting that phenomenon. In both New York and in Chicago, adults who created the new juvenile justice system were responding to a type of crime that simply did not exist when they themselves had been young. They did so within the framework of ideas that have formed the basis for our juvenile justice system since that time, but are under increasing attack today.

Notes

1. The report is partially reprinted in Wiley B. Sanders, ed., *Juvenile Offenders for a Thousand Years*, University of North Carolina Press, Chapel Hill, 1970, p. 102.

2. Bradford Kinney Peirce, *A Half Century with Juvenile Delinquents*, Patterson Smith, Montclair, 1969, pp. 32–38 (originally published in 1869).

3. Louise I. Shelley, *Crime and Modernization*, Southern Illinois University Press, Carbondale, IL, 1981, pp. 141–42.

4. Theodore N. Ferdinand, "Juvenile Delinquency or Juvenile Justice: Which Came First?" *Criminology* 27(1):79–106 (February, 1989), p. 84.

5. Robert H. Bremner, ed., *Children and Youth in America*. Vol. 1, Harvard University Press, Cambridge, 1970, p. 307.

6. Robert M. Mennel, *Thorns and Thistles: Juvenile Delinquents in the United States, 1825–1940*, University Press of New England, Hanover, NH, 1973, p. xxii.

7. Mennel, op. cit., p. xix; Bremner, op. cit., pp. 64, 104, 263.

8. Mennel, op. cit., p. xxii.

9. Bremner, op. cit., p. 262.

10. Mennell, op. cit., p. xxiv.

11. Mennel, op. cit., p. xxv; Bremner, op. cit., p. 307; Ferdinand, op. cit., p. 84.

12. Howard Zehr, *Crime and Development of Modern Society*, Rowman and Littlefield, Totowa, NJ, 1976. For an account of violence among primitive peoples and its decline in the modern world, see Martin Daly and Margo Wilson, *Homicide*, Aldine de Greuter, New York, 1988, Chapter 10.

13. For a brief history relevant to crime, see Raymond J. Michalowski, *Order, Law and Crime*, Random House, New York, 1985, pp. 84–85.

14. Jerome Hall, *Theft, Law and Society*, Bobbs-Merrill, Indianapolis, 1952.

15. Lawrence E. Cohen and Marcus Felson, "Social Change and Crime Rate Trends, A Routine Activity Approach," *American Sociological Review* 44:588–608 (August, 1979).

16. The beginning stages of industrialization also resulted in a temporary increase in violent crime, which further contributed to the perception that there was a crime wave. See Ted Robert Gurr, "Historical Forces in Violent Crime," in Michael Tonry and Norval Morris, eds., *Crime and Justice*, Vol. 3, University of Chicago Press, Chicago, 1981, p. 344; Shelley, op. cit. Violent crime later resumed its long-term downward trend.

17. Gideon Sjoberg, "The Origin and Evolution of Cities," in *Cities: Their Origin, Growth, and Human Impact*, Freeman, San Francisco, 1973, p. 19.

18. Kingsley Davis, "The Evolution of Western Industrial Cities," in *Cities, Their Origin, Growth, and Human Impact*, op. cit., p. 100.

19. David J. Rothman, *The Discovery of the Asylum*, Little, Brown, Boston, 1971, p. 12.

20. Carl Bridenbaugh, *Cities in Revolt*, Knopf, New York, 1955, p. 5.

21. Davis, op. cit.

22. Davis, op. cit.

23. Josef W. Konvitz, *The Urban Millennium*, Southern Illinois University Press, Carbondale, 1985, p. 77.

24. Ibid., p. 96.

25. Peirce, op. cit., p. 41.

26. Ferdinand, op. cit., p. 83.

27. Mennel, op. cit., p. xix.

28. Gurr, op. cit., pp. 345–46. For example, the changing proportions of males aged 15 to 29 between 1801 and 1971 in London's population trace a path that is quite similar to the changing volume of felonies in that city over those years. See Ted Robert Gurr, Peter N. Gradosky, and Richard C. Hula, *The Politics of Crime and Conflict*, Sage, Beverly Hills, 1977, p. 43.

29. Gurr, op. cit.

30. Ferdinand, op. cit.

31. Philippe Aries, *Centuries of Childhood*, Knopf, New York, 1962.

32. Aries, op. cit., p. 38.

33. Arlene Skolnick, *The Intimate Environment*, Little, Brown, New York, 1973, p. 333.

34. Lawrence Stone, "The Massacre of the Innocents, *The New York Review* 14:25–31 (November, 1974).

35. The "negative" aspects of the first conception of childhood are emphasized in the discussion by LaMar Empey, *American Delinquency*, Dorsey, Homewood, IL, 1982, Chs. 2–3.

36. Aries, op. cit., pp. 330–412. See also Lloyd de Mause, *The History of Childhood*, Psychohistory Press, New York, 1974.

37. Joseph E. Illick, "Child Rearing in Seventeenth Century England and America," in Lloyd de Mause, ed., op. cit., pp. 316–17.

38. Donovan, op. cit., p. 67.

39. Joseph F. Kett, *Rites of Passage*, Basic Books, New York, 1977; John Demos and Virginia Demos, "Adolescence in Historical Perspective," *Journal of Marriage and the Family*, 31:632–38 (1969).

5

The Origin of Juvenile Justice—
The First Juvenile Institution

The chapter examines New York City around the year 1825, when the first modern juvenile institution opened. It provides a specific example of the general process described in the last chapter; that is, it tells how a new term emerged to describe a new phenomenon. The term itself described a new idea, a new way of interpreting and understanding offending behavior by juveniles. That new idea became the basis for new organizations—the first juvenile institutions.

There is a saying: "Sometimes you can't see the forest for the trees." When you are in a forest, you are so close to it that you can only see individual trees, not the larger patterns and shapes of the forest itself. A person flying over the forest in a plane, in contrast, can see the forest much better but cannot see the trees as well.

The people we study in this chapter were embedded in their historical context. Like a person in a forest, they could see smaller events very easily, but could not see the larger patterns and shapes very well. We observe these people from the vantage point provided by one hundred seventy-five years, like people flying over a forest in an airplane. While we may miss many details, it is easier for us to recognize the larger patterns and shapes of history.

Historical Context: New York City Around 1820

In 1820, the leaders of the United States were mainly Protestant gentle-men who had been born before the American revolution into prominent and wealthy families in small, tightly knit towns. For example, imagine one such leader who was 65 years old in 1820. That man would have been born in 1755, when a large majority of towns in the United States had fewer than 1,000 people, and only a few places had more than 2,500.[1] New York City had fewer than 15,000 people in that year.[2]

That man would have been 21 years old in 1776 when the Declaration of Independence was signed, and 34 years old in 1789 when the United States Constitution was ratified. By 1820, when the man was 65 years old, the population of New York City was about 120,000 and was growing rapidly in response to immigration.[3] It was rapidly becoming a modern city: densely inhabited and increasingly chaotic, with many different racial and ethnic groups. But it was governed by these well-born Protestant gentlemen who had grown up in quiet and orderly small towns where people were pretty much the same and everyone knew their place and kept to it.

This was the beginning of the transformation of America from a rural and agricultural society into an urban and industrial society. From our vantage point today, we can see the larger patterns and shapes of the changes that were going on. But they could not see the forests for the trees. Like the fish in the water, they were immersed within these changes. All that they knew was that they had fought and died to establish a new and noble nation, and now things were breaking down:

> Something had gone wrong. Young ruffians ran in gangs though the streets, and watchmen found hungry urchins asleep under doorsteps. Beggars and cutpurses jostled the wealthy on busy thoroughfares. It had been less than fifty years since the supposedly perfect nation had been devised, but the noble plans of the forefathers already seemed in jeopardy. Even while the blood of life still coursed through the veins of Thomas Jefferson and John Adams, the perfect experiment seemed on its way to destruction.[4]

In the small, tightly knit towns in which these well-bred gentlemen had been born and raised, it was natural for prominent citizens to come together into voluntary associations to resolve community problems.[5] So when New York City began to experience these problems, these promi-nent gentlemen gathered to discuss what might be done.

The Society for the Prevention of Pauperism

Faced with a disturbing breakdown of quiet and orderliness, a meeting was held on December 16, 1817, at the request of John Griscom, a "Professor of Chemistry and Natural Philosophy" and Thomas Eddy, a financier who had been instrumental in building the Erie Canal. Both were Quakers interested in prison reform.[6]

The group constituted itself into a "Society for the Prevention of Pauperism," and appointed a committee to write "a statement of the prevailing causes of pauperism, with suggestions relative to the most suitable and efficient remedies." They met again two months later when "a full and elaborate report was made upon the causes and remedies of pauperism."

Paupers as "Undeserving" Poor People

The problem was defined as pauperism, not as poverty or crime or delinquency. Paupers were "undeserving" poor people—those undeserving of charity because of their wicked and dissolute ways. Paupers were deceitful, traitorous, hostile, rude, brutal, rebellious, sullen, wasteful, cowardly, dirty, and blasphemous. Paupers were lazy and refused to work, they got drunk and passed out in the gutters, they stole things and got into fights with each other, and they let their children run around without proper care and supervision.

Prominent citizens at the time generally believed that paupers were poor *because* they were corrupt and vice-ridden. That is, paupers became poor because they were deceitful, traitorous, hostile, rude, brutal, and so on. If they were honest and hard-working, then they would earn an adequate livelihood and would not be poor.

There were, of course, some people who were poor through no fault of their own. These were the "deserving" poor, the poor who were "deserving" of any charity that the wealthy elite of a small town might provide. An example would be the God-fearing widow who scrubbed laundry all night and then gathered up her eight small children to take them to church in the morning.

Such people were poor but they were not a problem—as the Bible says, "The poor you have always with you." The problem was pauperism. Paupers were poor people who had a whole list of nasty characteristics, and were poor precisely because of those characteristics. They were the reason that New York City was descending into chaos. In the "good old days," the law-abiding citizens would run those people out of town. But suddenly, in New York City, thousands of these paupers were cluttering up the streets, too many to run out of town. Something would have to be done.

The Reports on Pauperism

The first report to the Society was presented in February 1818, and focused on the conditions in New York City's penitentiaries. Twenty years earlier, Thomas Eddy, one of the two Quakers who called the meeting about paupers, organized the construction of the first penitentiary in New York City and served as its first warden.[7] Prisoners worked in silence, making goods to be sold to pay for their keep. They could also save any additional money they made.

However, free merchants thought this was unfair competition, so a law was passed in 1801 that required all goods to be labelled as prison-made.[8] Sales dropped off dramatically, and things quickly went downhill. In 1802, a major riot occurred that had to be put down by the military. Conditions continued to deteriorate, and Eddy decided the penitentiary had been a bad idea.

A second report, written in 1819, called attention to the fact that there were no separate facilities for juveniles in these penitentiaries. This was followed by a third report, written by Cadwallader Colden, who was mayor of New York and presiding Judge of the municipal court[9] (remember, New York only had 120,000 people at this time). Colden was particularly concerned that many youths came before his court who had not received proper care from their parents and were charged with relatively minor offenses. Juries would refuse to convict these youths because of their age, but Colden believed that this encouraged the youths to commit more crime. When they were convicted and sent to the penitentiary, however, Colden believed they were harmed by association with adult criminals. Colden concluded that, for these youths, "the penitentiary cannot but be a fruitful source of pauperism, a nursery of new vices and crimes, a college for the perfection of adepts in guilt."[10]

The fourth report, issued in 1822, took the natural step of recommending the establishment of a separate penitentiary for juvenile offenders.

But they also took a second natural step. This was a society for the *prevention* of pauperism, so they suggested that the new institution focus on the reform of the offenders, not punishment of offenses:

> These prisons should be rather schools for instruction than places for punishment like our present State prisons. . . . The wretchedness and misery of the offender should not be the object of the punishment inflicted; the end should be his reformation and future usefulness.[11]

The focus on prevention was advanced further by Thomas Eddy, who suggested that they bring in youths who had not committed any offenses but were in danger of doing so:

> European institutions had been constructed for young criminals, but no one had secured the power from the State of withdrawing, from the custody of weak or criminal parents, children who were vagabonds in the streets and in peril of a criminal life, although no overt act had been committed. The mayor [Colden] well remarks: "Deprived of this power, the institution would lose much of its influence."[12]

This focus on prevention, particularly the focus on juveniles who had not yet committed any crime, was the unique contribution of the New York House of Refuge, and why we consider this institution as the origin of the modern juvenile justice system.

The New York House of Refuge

The society renamed itself the *Society for the Reformation of Juvenile Delinquents,*[13] and developed plans for establishing a "house of refuge" for children in danger of growing up to be paupers and criminals. This first juvenile institution, called the New York House of Refuge, was opened on New Year's Day, 1825, at the present site of Madison Square Garden. At the time, this was about a mile beyond the last houses in the city and "was surrounded by cultivated farms, groves, open and rough fields blooming in their season with wild flowers."[14]

Juvenile Penitentiary or Juvenile Poorhouse?

This institution received few, if any, youths who would have been sent to the penitentiary. For example, nine of the first sixteen children sent to the

House of Refuge had not committed any punishable offense at all.[15] By the end of its first year, the House of Refuge had received a total of seventy-three children.[16] The most serious offender had been convicted of grand larceny. Nine additional children had been sent for petty larceny, and the remaining sixty-three for vagrancy, stealing, and running away from the poorhouse.

Of the youths who had committed punishable offenses, most would not have been sent to the penitentiary because of the reluctance of juries to convict them. Later in 1825, the New York City District Attorney stated in a speech at the House of Refuge:

> Before the establishment of the House, a lad of fourteen or fifteen years of age might have been arrested and then tried four or five times for petty thefts, and it was hardly ever that a jury would convict. They would rather that the culprit, acknowledged to be guilty, should be discharged altogether, than be confined in the prisons of our State and county. This rendered the lad more bold in guilt, and I have known instances of lads, now in the House, being indicted half a dozen times, and as often discharged to renew the crimes, and with the conviction that they might steal with impunity.[17]

Because there were few genuinely criminal youth, Rendlemen has argued that the House of Refuge really was a juvenile poorhouse rather than a juvenile penitentiary: an institution for poor youths who were in danger of growing up to be paupers.[18] Regardless of whether one agrees with that argument, almost all the children sent to this first House of Refuge were poor, but most of those same children were not criminal.

Two practices in the House of Refuge were consistent with practices in poorhouses. First, these juveniles were not sentenced for a certain length of time, proportionate to their offense, as in criminal courts. Rather, boys were committed until their twenty-first birthday and girls until their eighteenth birthday (this was later amended to be the same as the boys).[19] Second, commitment to the institution did not require a criminal conviction. A city alderman could simply issue an order admitting the youth, or a parent could apply to the board of the House of Refuge.[20]

Also consistent with the practice in poorhouses was the heavy emphasis on work.[21] Commentators on the children in the House of Refuge emphasized the connection between idleness and temptation:

> These children come to the institution almost universally heedless and indolent. They have never been put to serious labor, and seem almost to have

lost the capacity of entering upon any work requiring intelligence and skill. This condition of mind has rendered their attendance upon school almost profitless, even if they have been sent. . . .

Indolence is the mother of ignorance and impiety. It is the aimlessness and helplessness of these vagrant children than make them so certainly the victims of temptation. Every inmate leaving a reformatory should be able to say: *I learned to work there.*" (Emphasis in original.)[22]

The opening paragraph of the first "rules and regulations" of the House of Refuge stated:

The introduction of labor into the House of Refuge, will be regarded principally with reference to the moral benefits to be derived from it. If the employment should be unproductive of much pecuniary profit, still the gain to the city and State will eventually prove considerable, from the reformation and consequently the reduced number of offenders.[23]

The children therefore worked for eight hours per day at chair-making, tailoring, brass-nail manufacturing, and silver-plating, in addition to four hours per day for school.[24]

The Causes and Cures of Pauperism and Crime

The reformers believed that there were three possible causes of the problems of pauperism and crime among these juveniles: "weak and criminal parents," "the manifold temptations of the streets," and "the peculiar weakness of (the children's) moral nature."[25] The House of Refuge addressed all three problems by removing the children from their parents and from the streets, and by placing them in a highly disciplined program to reinforce their weak moral natures. Thus, the reformers believed that the House of Refuge would successfully cure delinquency.

The reformers, however, tended to focus on the inadequacies in the parent and the child, as opposed to the temptations of the streets, since so many of the urban poor were recent immigrants whereas the gentlemen reformers themselves were native-born Americans. The gentlemen reformers tended to see these immigrants as inferior. This tendency was exacerbated when the great Irish immigration took place as a result of the potato famine in the 1840s. Most of the gentlemen reformers were of English extraction, and they looked down on the Irish. In addition, they were Protestant, whereas the Irish immigrants were Catholics. The children of these Irish Catholic immigrants soom came to dominate the

House of Refuge,[26] and the gentlemen reformers naturally understood this as a reflection of the inferior racial stock of the Irish, who were placed under difficult circumstances by the "manifold temptations of the streets."

The managers were satisfied that the House of Refuge would cure this malady. In their fourth yearly report, the managers described their many successes:

> In almost every case, we do not say in all cases, the discipline of the institution works a reformation. The moral faculties are awakened, the thoughts of the young offender are turned, often with regret, upon his past life, and he is led to resolve on a better course. In many instances, the child not only thinks of his future condition in this world, but his mind is filled with a concern for his eternal as well as his temporal welfare; a conviction is produced that our happiness in this life, as well as in that which is to come, depends on a due application of our moral and physical faculties. The transition of a hopelessness, to the enjoyments in the Refuge of comfort, to the relief which is afforded to the mind by constant and useful employment, to the knowledge of good and evil, to the hope of obtaining an honest living, and to the consolations of religion, must be to him as a new birth.[27]

The "Placing Out" System

There was such a great supply of these potential paupers that the House of Refuge was soon filled and the question arose of what to do with them. Even though they were all committed until they turned 21, "it was never proposed to retain their inmates longer than to become satisfied of their reformation."[28] Yet sending them back to "the streets" clearly was a bad idea.

By 1828, only three years after founding the House of Refuge, the practice developed of sending youths to work on farms in newly settled states such as Ohio, Indiana, and Illinois. This was consistent with practices in poorhouses, which had been apprenticing out poor youths since around the year 1600.[29] However, it never had been associated with penitentiaries. This again supports the argument that the original house of refuge was really a poorhouse for juveniles, rather than a penitentiary.

The House of Refuge quickly became a shipping station for poor children who were thought to be in danger of growing up to be paupers. They would be removed from their families and would spend about a year in the House of Refuge learning good work habits. They then would be placed on trains headed west, where they would be indentured out for service until they reached 21. These apprenticeships soon accounted for 90% of releases from the House of Refuge, with the remainder consisting of deaths, escapes, transfers to adult prisons, and a few outright releases.[30]

This function was later taken over by the Children's Aid Society. For example, in 1854, they took forty-six boys and girls on a train to a church in a small town in Michigan. The Society's journal recorded what happened:

> At the close of the sermon the people were informed of the object of the Children's Aid Society. It met with cordial approval of all present and several promised to take the children. . . . Monday morning the boys held themselves in readiness to receive application from the farmers . . . and before Saturday they were all gone.[31]

In other places, the children would all get off the train in a particular town, where they would be picked over by local farmers. Those who were not chosen would get back on the train and move on to the next town.

Over 50,000 children were removed from New York City in this way.[32] Most of the time, there was no investigation of the family prior to the "placement," nor any check on how the child was treated afterward. Many children were never heard from again. Many others became problems in their new homes, either because they were problems to begin with or because they were so badly treated. Later on, many Western states passed laws forbidding this practice, or requiring that the Children's Aid Society post a bond for each child to ensure that the child did not become a public burden.

The natural parents were not usually told where the child had ended up, nor were they allowed any further contact with the child since they were usually seen as the original source of the problem. Managers sent glowing reports to the parents about how healthy and happy the children were, but recent historical research has turned up pitiful letters from the children about terrible conditions under which they lived.[33] These letters were not forwarded to the parents.

Juvenile Delinquency vs. Potential Pauperism

Perhaps the best way to understand this new institution is to realize that the original idea of juvenile delinquency was derived from and merged with the earlier idea of pauperism. Although the terms sound quite different, at the time they had almost identical meanings.

The literal meaning of the term "delinquency" refers to a neglect or failure to perform tasks required by law or duty. For example, people are "delinquent" in their taxes when they fail to pay them on time. That meaning is quite similar to the meaning of the term "pauper," which refers to a poor person who neglects or fails to perform the tasks required by law and duty in society: hard, honest work.

While the term "delinquency" is quite similar to the term "pauperism," the term "juvenile" is derived from the second idea of childhood and essentially means a "potential adult." Considered literally, a "juvenile delinquent" is a certain kind of potential adult: a potential adult who will neglect or fail to perform the hard, honest work required by law and duty.

Because the idea of "juvenile delinquency" was very similar to the idea of "potential pauperism," the procedures for handling juvenile delinquents resembled the procedures that had long been used to handle potential paupers. Since at least the Poor Law of 1601 in England, young paupers from urban areas had been taken into poorhouses and then apprenticed out to rural areas.[34] This practice was transplanted to the American colonies, and was in frequent and customary use.[35] With the establishment of the House of Refuge, the same practice continued, directed at the same poor population and with the same intent: to ensure that these poor youths grew up to become honest, hard workers instead of paupers.

Part of the reason that juvenile delinquency as an idea and the House of Refuge as an institution were so successful is that they fit comfortably into the ideas and practices of the day. Although it sounded like a new and different and promising idea at the time, the idea of juvenile delinquency was really a minor variation on the old and well-established idea of potential pauperism. While it seemed like a new and different and promising practice, the House of Refuge was really a minor variation on the old and well-established practice of placing potential paupers from urban areas into a poorhouse for a period of time and then apprenticing them out to rural areas where they could learn the benefits of honest, hard work.

Legal Issues Related to the Juvenile Institutions

The Case of Mary Ann Crouse

The idea of the House of Refuge spread quickly. A second house was established in Boston in 1826 (one year after the first one in New York) and a third in Philadelphia the following year.

One girl sent to the Philadelphia House of Refuge was named Mary Ann Crouse. Like many others, she had not committed any criminal offense, but was a poor child who appeared to be in danger of growing up to become a pauper. On the complaint of her mother, she was brought into court and committed to the House of Refuge. Her father objected to this and filed a writ of *habeus corpus* (a legal demand for the state to explain why it is holding someone).

Mary Ann's father raised a crucial legal issue. A very basic principle of criminal law is that there should be no punishment unless a crime has been committed. But Mary Ann had not committed any crime. Her father argued that the state had no right to punish her, so she should be released.

The case went to the Pennsylvania Supreme Court, which handed down its opinion in 1838. In it, the court rejected the father's arguments and held that sending Mary Ann to the House of Refuge was perfectly legal:

> The object of the charity is reformation, by training its inmates to industry; by imbuing their minds with principles of morality and religion; by furnishing them with means to earn a living; and, above all, by separating them from the corrupting influence of improper associates. To this end, may not the natural parents, when unequal to the task of education, or unworthy of it, be superseded by the *parens patriae,* or common guardian of the community? . . . The infant has been snatched from a course which must have ended in confirmed depravity; and not only is the restraint of her person lawful, but it would be an act of extreme cruelty to release her from it.[36]

Four points in this quotation form the basis of the decision. Each is important for later developments in the juvenile justice system.

First, the court argued that Mary Ann was being *helped, not punished.* The House of Refuge was a charitable school, not a prison. The object of the House was to save her from a terrible fate, not to punish her for criminal offenses. The question of whether children in juvenile institutions are being punished or helped is one that will come up again and again in the history of the juvenile justice system.

Second, the court focused on the *good intentions* of those who ran the House of Refuge, as compared to the *actual performance* of Mary Ann's parents. In fact, by 1838, the juvenile institutions had already abandoned most elements of rehabilitation and had become heavily oriented toward custody. The rigid routine was marked by numerous escape attempts and inmate uprisings, which were followed by whippings and leg irons and cold showers in the middle of winter.[37] If the court had compared the actual performance of the House of Refuge with the good intentions of Mary Ann's parents, it might have reached the opposite decision. The comparison of good intentions versus actual performance is one that will be made several more times in the legal history of the juvenile justice system.

Third, the court argued that it was legal to "help" Mary Ann because of the state's role as *"parens patriae."*[38] This Latin phrase means "parent of the country," and it was originally used in the 1500s in England in connection with children whose parents had died, leaving an estate. In such cases, a special court (called Chancery Court) would manage the estate until it could be turned over to the child at the age of 21. This was done on the theory that, when the child's natural parents were dead, the state, as parent of the country ("parens patriae"), would take over the role of the child's parent.

The case of Mary Ann Crouse was the first where this concept was applied to a poor child whose parents were still alive, rather than to a (presumably wealthy) child whose parents had died and left an estate. There was a certain similarity: in the one case, the parents were dead, while in the other, the parents were "unequal to the task of education, or unworthy of it."

Sixty years later, the concept of "parens patriae" would become the legal foundation of the first juvenile court. The question of whether "parens patriae" was a legitimate or appropriate rationale for sending children to institutions, however, would continue to be debated.

Fourth, because the Pennsylvania Supreme Court held that Mary Ann was not being punished, it also held that she did not need any protections of *formal due process* granted to defendants in a criminal trial. One of those protections was the legal doctrine that there should be no punishment without a crime. Mary Ann had been brought into a criminal court and sent to an institution when she had not committed any crime. But the court held that she was not being punished at all, so that it did not matter that she had not committed a crime. The question of whether juveniles are entitled to the formal protections of due process is one that will continue to be raised in legal cases involving the juvenile justice system.

This was the first legal challenge to an increasingly widespread practice: children who had not committed any criminal offense were brought into criminal court and committed to a House of Refuge until they were 21 years old. This was part of Thomas Eddy's original idea in his proposal to establish the New York House of Refuge. While the court upheld the practice in this case, another case arose thirty years later that produced the opposite result.

The Case of Daniel O'Connell

By 1868, over twenty houses of refuge sprang up all over the country, and through the years they housed between 40,000 and 50,000 youths.[39] After 1850, however, the apprenticing system began to break down, and it became harder and harder to place children in jobs when they were released.[40] Accordingly, the number of outright discharges increased, and children were simply sent back to their homes. Increasing levels of violence occurred in the Houses of Refuge, and in general they were no longer seen in such an idealized glow.

One of the newer Houses of Refuge had been established in Chicago, and through its doors came a boy named Daniel O'Connell. Like Mary Ann Crouse, he had not committed any criminal offense, but appeared to be in danger of growing up to become a pauper and was committed to the school until his twenty-first birthday. Daniel's parents objected and, like Mary Ann's father, filed a writ of *habeus corpus*.

This case went to the Illinois Supreme Court which ordered Daniel released in 1870.[41] Thus, they reached the opposite decision in a case almost identical to that of Mary Ann Crouse. The legal reasoning of that decision can be compared with the legal reasoning in the Crouse case on each of the four points described above.

First, in the O'Connell case, the Illinois Supreme Court concluded that Daniel was being *punished, not helped,* by being sent to the reform school:

> Why should minors be imprisoned for misfortune? Destitution of proper parental care, ignorance, idleness and vice, are misfortunes, not crimes. . . . This boy is deprived of a father's care; bereft of home influences; has no freedom of action; is committed for an uncertain time; is branded as a prisoner; made subject to the will of others, and thus feels he is a slave.[42]

Recall that the Pennsylvania Surpreme Court took the opposite stance: that Mary Ann was being helped, not punished, by being sent to the House of Refuge.

Second, the O'Connell court described the harsh realities of the Chicago Reform School, but seemed to grant the benefit of the doubt to Daniel's parents, who were presumed to care for the boy and want to provide good "home influences." That is, the O'Connell court compared the *actual performance* of the Chicago Reform School with the *good intentions* of Daniel's parents. The Pennsylvania Supreme Court had taken the opposite stance, describing the House of Refuge in idealistic terms but Mary Ann's parents in harsh ones. This change reflected the fact that reform schools were now almost fifty years old and much of the idealism about them had faded.

Third, the Illinois Supreme Court rejected the *parens patriae* doctrine as the basis for dealing with juveniles. The Illinois Supreme Court simply viewed Daniel as being "imprisoned," so their decision focused on legal doctrines related to criminal courts and criminal punishments.[43] The doctrine of "parens patriae," and related concepts like chancery courts and the "best interests" of children, were irrelevant and did not enter into the decision.

Fourth, once the idealized and romanticized version of the House of Refuge was discarded, then the need for the *formal due process* protections was obvious:

Can the State, as parens patriae, exceed the power of the natural parent, except in punishing crime? These laws provide for the "safe keeping" of the child; they direct his "commitment" and only a "ticket of leave" or the uncontrolled discretion of a board of guardians, will permit the imprisoned boy to breathe the pure air of heaven outside his prison walls. . . . The confinement may be from one to fifteen years, according to the age of the child. Executive clemency cannot open the prison doors for no offense has been committed. The writ of *habeas corpus,* a writ for the security of liberty, can afford no relief, for the sovereign power of the State as parens patriae has determined the imprisonment beyond recall. Such restraint upon natural liberty is tyranny and oppression. If, without crime, without the conviction of an offense, the children of the State are thus to be confined for the "good of Society," then Society had better be reduced to its original elements and free government acknowledged a failure. . . . Even criminals cannot be convicted and imprisoned without due process of law.[44]

Similarities Between the Two Cases

The similarities and differences in these two cases can be summed up in Table 2.

TABLE 2. A Comparison Between the Crouse and O'Connell Cases

	Crouse case	*O'Connell case*
Court focused on	Good intentions	Actual performance
Juveniles were said to be	Helped and treated	Punished
Legal basis of court's decision	Parens patriae	Criminal law
Decision	Due process is not required	Due process is required

What is remarkable, given the fact that they reached opposite decisions, is that these two cases presented the judges with virtually identical sets of facts. Neither juvenile had committed a criminal offense, but both were committed to a juvenile institution until they were 21. Both fathers sought release of their child by filing a writ of *habeus corpus*. Each case went to the state Supreme Court, where opposite decisions were reached.

These opposite decisions were reached because the judges in the case had two contrasting "ideas of juvenile justice." These two contrasting "ideas" continue to struggle for the soul of juvenile justice today.

The Crouse court warmly viewed the House of Refuge in a rosy glow, while coldly glaring at the inadequacies of Mary Ann's parents. They concluded that she was being helped by the House of Refuge, that she did not need to be protected from this help by the formal requirements of due process, and that the legal basis for all of this was the *parens patriae* doctrine that the state could step in as parent when the natural parents failed in their role. While so strong a stance is rarely taken today, many people view the juvenile justice in essentially similar terms.

The O'Connell court, in contrast, coldly glared at the inadequacies of the Chicago Reform School but cast warm glances in the direction of the (supposedly) loving parents. They concluded that Daniel was being treated like a criminal even though he had not committed a crime. The legal protections of formal due process therefore were as important to him as to an adult, and the doctrine of *parens patriae* was irrelevant. Many people continue to view juvenile justice in essentially similar terms today.

The Larger Impact of These Cases

These two cases are directly comparable to two later cases in which all the same arguments were repeated—the Fisher case in 1905 repeats the arguments made in the Crouse case, and the Gault case in 1967 repeats the arguments made in the O'Connell case. Because Gault is the most recent case, you might conclude that O'Connell-type reasoning has won this particular debate.

But both lines of reasoning are legally adequate, so that a new Crouse-type decision could be handed down in the future. In fact, I argue in chapter 8 that we should expect such a decision unless we break our present cycle of juvenile justice. The same conditions that led to the Crouse decision and later to the Fisher decision are going to emerge again, at which time a similar decision is likely to appear.

The O'Connell case set the stage for the founding of the first juvenile court in Chicago in 1899. The judge had ruled that it was illegal to send poor children to reform schools unless they had committed a felony offense. As a result of that case, "by 1890 the Illinois system of handling delinquent children, haphazard at best, had virtually evaporated."[45]

Many people at the time believed that sending poor children to institutions, even though they had committed no crime, had been a good practice and was best for the children themselves. The O'Connell ruling therefore outlawed a practice that they thought was good and right and just and important. These people went looking for a new legal basis to continue this practice, even though the court had defined it as illegal. They created that new legal basis by founding the first juvenile court.

Essentially, the juvenile court was invented to get around the O'Connell ruling. It allowed Illinois once again to send to juvenile institutions poor children who had not committed a criminal offense. Thus, the juvenile court did not establish a new and different way of doing things. It allowed Illinois to return to its old way of doing things, after that way had been declared illegal by the courts.

The Lessons of History

Why Did the House of Refuge "Sell"?

"Juvenile delinquency" as an idea and the House of Refuge as a practice spread quickly throughout the country. They did not solve the problem of urban property crime by lower-class youths, but they did win the competition with other interpretations of this phenomenon and other ways of responding to it. As such, they became the basis of the present juvenile justice system while other ideas and other reforms faded away, leaving no trace in today's world.

We can ask why this particular idea and this particular reform were "successful" in their competition with other possible ideas and reforms. Other ideas besides "juvenile delinquency" can be used for understanding and interpreting urban property crime by lower-class youths. There also are other mechanisms besides a "house of refuge" for responding to this phenomenon. Why did this particular idea and this particular policy "succeed" at the time and become the basis for our modern juvenile justice system? Phrased bluntly, why did this idea and reform "sell" better than other ideas and other reforms?

The Cycle of Juvenile Justice

The problem faced by these gentlemen reformers fits into the "cycle of juvenile justice," as described in Chapter 2. High juvenile crime rates were accompanied by a firm belief that this had not been a problem back in the "good old days." Harsh punishments were available, but reluctance of officials to impose them meant that many youths were let off scot-free. Officials at the time, such as Mayor Colden, thought both of these choices increased juvenile crime.

The House of Refuge was designed to provide a middle ground between punishing harshly and doing nothing at all. It offered leniency for those who would have been harshly punished, and it also provided some response for those juveniles who would have been released scot-free. In terms of "criminal justice thermodynamics,"[46] the House of Refuge reduced the severity of the penalty so as to increase the frequency of its application.

Thus, one piece of the cycle seems to have existed at the time of this reform. If the "cycle" itself exists, then we can expect to find that juvenile crime rates remain high despite the introduction of leniency and that many people remain convinced that they can be reduced through appropriate justice policies. These people soon conclude that high crime rates are caused by leniency. They gradually "toughen up" the response to delinquency until only harsh punishments are available. At that point, justice officials again find themselves in the position of choosing between imposing harsh punishments or doing nothing at all. Juvenile crime rates remain high and now are attributed to the forced choice between two bad alternatives. At some point, a new reform reintroduces leniency in order to solve this problem, and the cycle starts over.

The Idea of Juvenile Delinquency: Potential Pauper

The idea of "juvenile delinquency," as originally proposed by the gentlemen reformers in New York City, sounded new and different and exciting and promising. But it really was a slightly revised version of the old and popular idea that poor youths were "potential paupers." Considered literally, the two terms have almost identical meanings.

One reason that the idea of "juvenile delinquency" was popular was that it sounded new and different but it actually wasn't. It did not require people to think anything different from what they had thought in the past. Fitting comfortably into the historical and philosophical context of the day, people got all the satisfactions of believing that they were taking an entirely new way of looking at things, but none of the trouble and inconvenience of actually grappling with new concepts and ideas.

The Idea of Juvenile Justice: House of Refuge

The House of Refuge as a method for responding to delinquents also seemed new and different and exciting and promising. Because it seemed so innovative, people were optimistic about how effective it would be in solving the problems of delinquency. In fact, however, the House of Refuge was a slightly modified version of the old and well-established method for handling pauper youths in the past—put them in an institution for a period of time and then apprentice them out to rural areas where they work on farms until they become adults. Like the new idea of juvenile delinquency, the House of Refuge was probably popular in part because it sounded new and different but it actually wasn't.

The House of Refuge did establish a new legal basis for the old practice of sending poor urban children to institutions for their own good, and then apprenticing them out to rural areas until they reached the age of 21. The old legal basis was found in "poor laws," but these had begun to wither away and had more or less disappeared by the end of the 1800s.[47] The new legal basis for this practice was found in the thinking in the Crouse decision. Thus, the practice was able to survive and grow at the same time that its legal basis was dying.

Economic Interests of the Rich and Powerful

The reformers believed that delinquency had three causes: "the peculiar weaknesses of (the children's) moral natures," "weak and criminal parents," and "the manifold temptations of the streets." From our perspective, it seems that the major problem was in the "streets" rather than in the parents or children—that is, in the conditions under which poor parents and children lived.

Poor parents and children found themselves in a new historical situation: the beginning of urbanization and industrialization. We now know that every time this historical situation occurs, the modern problem of juvenile delinquency soon follows.[48] Thus, it seems reasonable to conclude that these parents and children probably were no "weaker" or "more criminal" than parents and children at other times and other places where no such problem of delinquency appeared.

The House of Refuge, as a reform, did not attempt to change "the streets" in any way. Instead, it attempted to remove from the streets children who had "weak moral natures" and "weak and criminal parents." Its major thrust was to compensate for these supposed weaknesses in the child and the parent. Yet we can conclude today that these weaknesses were not the real problem.

Would it have been possible to change "the streets"—that is, the conditions under which poor people lived? To ask the question is likely to provoke protests that nothing could have been done anyway and so there is no point in thinking about it. I argue that this simply is not true.

It may be true that few options were available, and that if implemented those options would only have had a small impact on the way poor people lived. It may be true that there were few people who were willing to look at "the streets" as a cause of problems that might be solved. It may be true that taking this perspective would have violated fundamental philosophical and religious beliefs of powerful groups at the time, who would have thought it was almost treasonous. But it is also true that there were at least some things that could have been done at the time to improve the conditions under which poor people lived.

From our vantage point one hundred seventy-five years later, I would argue that juvenile delinquency as an idea and the House of Refuge as a policy response succeeded in part because they were "convenient" for rich and powerful people to believe. Other ideas and other policy responses, especially those that would have attempted to change the conditions under which poor people lived, would have been inconvenient in that they would have threatened the economic interests of those groups. These ideas were developing at the time, but they were not implemented because prominent and powerful people were unwilling to consider them.[49]

Moral and Intellectual Superiority of the Reformers

Reformers in New York City were confronted with a world they did not understand. There was an enormous social distance between the small group of prominent and powerful gentlemen who ran the city and the large number of poor immigrants with whom they were so concerned. Confronted with this uncertainty, the reformers chose to believe that in the complex and stressful environment of New York City, children with "peculiar weaknesses of moral nature" were being raised by "weak and criminal parents." Today, it seems reasonable to conclude that these weaknesses were not the problem. What was it about that particular interpretation that led these reformers to believe it rather than some other interpretation?

I suggest that this particular interpretation was popular because it reinforced a sense of moral and intellectual superiority among the reformers themselves. By believing that immigrant groups were morally inferior, the reformers were able to believe that they themselves were morally superior.[50] People always like to believe good things about themselves. How much better it must have felt to think that these people were morally inferior than to believe that their problems arose from social conditions that you and your friends created and maintained and profited from?

This sense of moral superiority then justified taking control of the situation, and led to a vast optimism about how effective their actions would be. They felt certain that everything they did would work out for the best.

The "Unfair Comparison"

Vast optimism is a natural reaction whenever people undertake a reform, particularly with difficult problems such as delinquency. Like today, people at that time wanted a "sure cure" for this problem.[51] They wanted to believe that everything would work out just fine, and tended to believe anyone who promised that it would.

As evident in the Crouse decision, this optimism was supported by focusing on the reformer's good intentions, and by assuming that the actual practices associated with those reforms would completely fulfill those intentions. The founders of the New York House of Refuge simply assumed that things would work out in practice according to their good intentions. If there were problems, it was just a question of working out the details. In their idealism, the reformers did not anticipate the many difficult and ultimately insoluble problems that would develop in these Houses.

Vast optimism about the future was further supported by making a comparison to a highly critical, pessimistic view of the policies in effect before the reform. This is a common practice for reformers, who usually emphasize the failures and inadequacies of past policies, portraying them as much worse than they really are. The pessimistic assessment of the past is based on the actual practices of past policies, where the good intentions of the people who implemented those policies are ignored.

The "unfair comparison," then, is a comparison between an optimistic, idealistic assessment of the future, based on the good intentions of the reformers, and a pessimistic, cynical assessment of the past, based on the actual performance of the policies. Structuring the comparison in this way fuels the drive for change.

This is the comparison that was found in both the Mary Ann Crouse and Daniel O'Connell cases. In the Crouse case, the good intentions of those running the House of Refuge were compared to the actual performance of Mary Ann's parents. In the O'Connell case, the actual performance of the Chicago Reform School was compared to the good intentions of Daniel's parents. In each case, this unfair comparison was used to justify the court's decision, whereas a fair comparison would have made the decision appear less certain and more problematical.

It is usually easy to make this unfair comparison at the time of a reform. Reformers propose new policies that are not yet implemented or have only just been implemented. Good intentions are in abundance, but actual practices are scarce. Thus, it is easy to gaze lovingly at the good intentions of reformers, while casting only an occasional sideways glance at what actually happens.

In contrast, past policies have been in effect for years, so the actual practices are apparent. In addition, whatever the lofty idealism present when those old policies were established has been worn down by the intractable problems the policies face, leaving cynical and burnt-out people as their advocates. Even if those people still have good intentions, they lack the fervor, excitement, and certainty that come with inexperience. Ignorance, after all, is bliss.

Combining optimism about the future and pessimism about the past is an additional way of demonstrating the reformers' moral and intellectual superiority. If the past was really that terrible and the future is really that bright, then the reformers who accomplished this change must be wonderous human beings deserving of the highest praise and admiration.

Expansion of State Power

Ultimately, the bright hopes for the future, based on moral superiority and good intentions of the reformers, justified an expansion of state power. The Pennsylvania Supreme Court found that Mary Ann Crouse did not need due process protections because she simply did not need to be protected from these noble, well-intentioned people. The reformers were granted this power because of an optimistic assessment that they would use it for Mary Ann's own good.

Expansion of state power therefore was linked to the optimism about how effective the House of Refuge was. The optimism itself was not justified by the actual performance of that institution, which had already degenerated substantially, but by the good intentions of its founders. When the O'Connell court later found that juveniles did need due process, it was because the court had looked at actual performance rather than at good intentions.

Reformers usually want to expand state power rather than limit it. They usually believe in their own ability to do good things and do not want their efforts to be restricted by laws and due process rights. How comfortable the Crouse decision must have felt with these reformers, so sure of their ability to do good. How uncomfortable the O'Connell decision must have felt, with its implication that Daniel needed protection from these very reformers.

Conclusion

If these lessons are correct, then we will find the same patterns at the time of the next reform—the founding of the first juvenile court in Chicago in 1899. Ultimately, the question to ask while reading the rest of this book is whether such lessons might apply today.

Notes

1. David J. Rothman, *The Discovery of the Asylum*, Little, Brown, Boston, 1971, p. 12.

2. Ibid., p. 13.

3. Bradford Kinney Peirce, *A Half Century with Juvenile Delinquents*, Patterson Smith, Montclair, 1969, p. 41 (originally published in 1869).

4. Robert S. Picket, *House of Refuge*, Syracuse University Press, Syracuse, 1969, pp. xviii–xix; quoted in Finestone, op. cit., p. 19.

5. For a discussion of the role of prominent gentlemen in colonial America, see Paul K. Longmore, *The Invention of George Washington*, University of California Press, Berkeley, 1988.

6. Peirce, op. cit., pp. 32–38.

7. Blake McKelvey, *American Prisons*, Patterson Smith, Montclair, 1977, p. 8.

8. Joseph J. Senna and Larry J. Siegel, *Introduction to Criminal Justice*, West, St. Paul, 1978, p. 366.

9. Peirce, op. cit., p. 40.

10. Ibid.

11. Peirce, op. cit., pp. 41–42.

12. Ibid., p. 34. See also p. 54.

13. Ibid., pp. 63, 65.

14. Ibid., p. 74.

15. Brenner, op. cit., p. 13.

16. Sanford Fox, "Juvenile Justice Reform: An Historical Perspective," *Stanford Law Review* 22:1187 (1970), p. 1192.

17. Peirce, op. cit., p. 79.

18. Douglas Rendleman, "Parens Patriae: From Chancery to the Juvenile Court," *South Carolina Law Review* 23:205 (1971); reprinted in Frederic L. Faust and Paul J. Brantingham, *Juvenile Justice Philosophy*, West, St. Paul, 1979, pp. 58–96.

19. Peirce, op. cit., p. 105.

20. Ibid., pp. 82–83.

21. A similar connection between prisons and productive labor has been documented in Dario Melossi and Massimo Pavarini, *The Prison and The Factory: Origins of the Penitentiary System*, Macmillan, London, 1979.

22. Peirce, op. cit., pp. 84–85.

23. Quoted in ibid., p. 86.

24. Ibid., p. 87.

25. Ibid., p. 82.

26. Harold Finestone, *Victims of Change,* Greenwood Press, Westport, CT, 1976, p. 31.

27. Peirce, op. cit., p. 110.

28. Ibid., p. 105.

29. Rendleman, op. cit., p. 62.

30. Mennel, op. cit., pp. 22–23.

31. Quoted in Walter I. Trattner, *From Poor Law to Welfare State,* Free Press, New York, 1974, p. 103.

32. Ibid., p. 104.

33. Brenner, op. cit., pp. 22–26. As late as 1894, an overseer of the poor in Pennsylvania was prosecuted for indenturing a 7-year-old boy to a cruel farmer. The overseer had been warned about the farmer and visited the boy after he was indentured, but did not find anything wrong. The boy died of starvation and overwork after only a few months. See *Commonwealth* v. *Coyle,* 160 Pa. 36, 28 A. 576, 28 A. 634 (1894), cited in Rendleman, op. cit., p. 63, ftn. 29.

34. Trattner, op. cit., pp. 10–12.

35. Stefan A. Riesenfield, "The Formative Era of American Public Assistance Law," *California Law Review* 43(2):175–233, 1955.

36. Mennel, op. cit., p. 14.

37. Mennel, op. cit., pp. 19–20. Mennel quotes a disgruntled former employee who wrote an "expose" about the place (p. 27). See also John Mahony's account of his experiences as a boy in the House of Refuge in Charles Sutton, *The New York Tombs,* The U.S. Publishing Company, New York, 1874, pp. 171–76; reprinted by Patterson-Smith, Montclair, NJ. Mahony describes how "my first promptings towards crime originated in the House of Refuge." He concludes: "I have been a prisoner in Sing Sing State Prison when it was at its worst, but, in many respects, I would rather be confined in Sing Sing than the House of Refuge, as the 'Refuge' was conducted when I was there."

38. Rendleman, op. cit.

39. Peirce, op. cit., p. 78.

40. Mennel, op. cit., p. 62.

41. *People* v. *Turner,* 55 Ill. 280 (1870).

42. Quoted in Mennel, op. cit., p. 125.

43. Only twelve years later, the same court reversed itself and approved, in a roundabout way, the concept of *parens patriae.* This was the *Ferrier* case (103 Ill. 367, 1882). Rendleman (op. cit., p. 82) states:

> The Illinois Supreme Court, by striking down the legislature's idea that poor children could be taken from their parents [in the *O'Connell* case], gave the onus to the legislature to develop an alternative. The legislature came back with more of the same and the court receded [in the *Ferrier* case].

44. Quoted in Platt, op. cit., pp. 103–04.

45. Mennel, op. cit., pp. 127–28.

46. Samuel Walker, *Sense and Nonsense About Crime,* Brooks/Cole, Pacific Grove, CA, 1989, pp. 46–48. See also pp. 36–37 above for a discussion of this concept.

47. Rendleman, op. cit.

48. Louise Shelley, *Crime and Modernization*, Southern Illinois University Press, Carbondale, 1981.

49. See Philip Jenkins, "Varieties of Enlightenment Criminology," *British Journal of Criminology* 24(2): 112–30 (April, 1984) for a discussion of more "radical" theories developing around that time.

50. In general, see Emile Durkheim on crime as "normal" in society, summarized in George B. Vold and Thomas J. Bernard, *Theoretical Criminology*, Oxford University Press, New York, 1986, pp. 146–50.

51. James O. Finkenauer, *Scared Straight! and the Panacea Phenomenon.* Prentice-Hall, Englewood Cliffs, NJ, 1982.

6

The Origin of Juvenile Justice—
The First Juvenile Court

Thomas Eddy had come up with the idea that children in danger of growing up to be paupers and criminals might be taken away from their parents (even though they had not committed any offense) and placed in institutions where they would be trained to be hard-working, God-fearing, law-abiding citizens. His idea spread throughout the country during the 1800s, but then was largely dismantled in Illinois due to the Daniel O'Connell decision in 1870. Many prominent and powerful people in that state favored this system and thus were in the market for a new legal mechanism for reestablishing it. They created it by founding the first juvenile court.

This new juvenile court was not a junior criminal court, as we think of it today. It was a social welfare agency, the central processing unit of the entire child welfare system. Children who had needs of any kind could be brought into the juvenile court, where their troubles would be diagnosed and the services they needed provided by court workers or obtained from other agencies.

One aspect was similar to criminal courts: the juvenile court had coercive powers. Other welfare agencies were voluntary, so that children or parents who did not wish to receive services could simply refuse them.

The new juvenile court, in contrast, was endowed with greater coercive powers than the criminal court. Parents and children had almost no ability to resist the court's efforts to help. With such great power in the service of so noble an undertaking, the founders of the juvenile court were certain that the problem of delinquency would soon be solved.

As in New York seventy-five years earlier, the views that led to the establishment of this court can only be understood by analyzing their context. We begin by looking at conditions in Chicago around the year 1900.

Historical Context: Chicago at the Turn of the Century

No city ever grew as rapidly as Chicago did in the 1800s.[1] A person who was born in Chicago in 1840 started life in a village of 5,000 people. By the time that person was 60 years old in 1900, Chicago was a gigantic metropolis of 1,500,000. This growth was fueled by wave upon wave of immigrants. In 1890, 70% of the people who lived in Chicago were born in foreign countries. Most of the rest were first-generation Americans whose parents were born abroad.

In this enormous city, only a small group of people had been in America for several generations, but this group controlled almost the entire political and business establishment in the city. Like the "gentlemen reformers" who founded the first juvenile institution in New York, this group was quite wealthy and almost all of them had been born in small towns or villages. Like those reformers, these people were profoundly disturbed at the breakdown of social order in the chaos that Chicago had become, and they focused their attention on the children, since the adults seemed to be lost causes. And like them, they generally believed that there were three "causes" of this disorder: weak and criminal parents, the manifold temptations of the streets, and the peculiar weakness of their moral natures.

The Latest Scientific Thinking

The latest scientific thinking of the day supported these general beliefs. In 1856, Darwin had first published his theory of evolution, and he applied that theory to human beings in 1871.[2] The theory that humans had evolved from lesser species rather quickly led to the view (called social

Darwinism) that some racial or ethnic groups of people were more highly evolved than others. In particular, the view became popular among white Anglo-Saxon Protestants that their group was the most highly evolved, and that other groups were biologically inferior.

In 1876, the Italian physician Lombroso used evolution to explain crime.[3] He argued that criminals were biological throwbacks to an earlier evolutionary state, that they were "less civilized" and more inclined to engage in violence and theft. This was called the theory of the "atavistic" criminal, and it became very popular among groups that considered themselves more highly evolved.

Thus, the latest thinking in evolution suggested that some people were less evolved than others, and the latest thinking in criminology suggested that less evolved people tended to commit more crime. As it happened, virtually all of the powerful people in Chicago were white Anglo-Saxon Protestants, while a great majority of the recent immigrants were not. This meant that, aside from other possible explanations, it could be argued that the crime and disorder resulted because these immigrant groups were biologically inferior.

This gave powerful people a sense of certainty in their own views, since they believed themselves superior and the other groups inferior. Unfortunately, this sense of certainty and superiority was combined with at least some ignorance about the supposedly inferior people. That ignorance was generated by the enormous social distance between the very small group of wealthy, native-born Americans who were in positions of power and the vast bulk of the poor immigrant population.[4]

The Position of Women

Where the first juvenile institution had been founded by men, the first juvenile court was largely the result of the work of women. Anthony Platt examined these women and presented a rather cynical view that illustrates the social distance, the sense of superiority, and the sense of certainty described above.[5]

According to Platt, these women were not progressives leading the charge for social reform. Such progressive women were active at the time and were being arrested and imprisoned for advocating such dangerous ideas as the use of birth control and allowing women to vote. In contrast, the women who founded the first juvenile court were relatively conservative. They primarily were the wives and daughters of prominent and powerful men who ran Chicago's political and business establishments. Like those men, they were wealthy, white, Anglo-Saxon, and Protestant. Like them, they had a sense of their own superiority and of their God-given and natural role at the peak of the social hierarchy.

These women were in a dilemma. They were energetic, educated, talented, perceptive, and believed that the wealthy had an obligation to return something to the larger society through public service. But they were also conservative and believed in the traditional women's role as related to home, family, and children. Finally, they were wealthy, with plenty of servants to cook and clean and raise their own children. Since their traditional women's role as the keeper of the house and hearth was taken care of by these servants, these women really had nothing to do.

This dilemma was solved when they began to address the problems of poor children. Taking care of children was at the heart of the traditional role for women. In this role, these wealthy women could go out from their homes into the larger society to use their energies, talents, and abilities without violating their own conservative sense of what is appropriate for women to do.

Initially, this allowed these women to go into the slums of Chicago to work with the children themselves. Ultimately, it allowed them to go before the City Council and State Legislature, arguing for major policy changes in handling of juvenile offenders. Unless the subject had been the problems of children, such involvement in the political process would have been utterly incompatible with their traditional role as women. Thus, taking on this problem had considerable benefits for them personally.

The First Juvenile Court

The Problem and the Solution

These women were confronted with a justice system that had, in their view, largely broken down. For most of the century, a "preventive" system had been taking poor children who were in danger of becoming paupers and criminals out of their homes and placing them in reform schools where they could be helped. But the system had been derailed by the Daniel O'Connell case, which declared the practice illegal. After that case, only children who had been convicted of felonies could be sent to reform school.[6] According to Richard Tuthill, who later became the first juvenile court judge, this decision "overthrew the whole prospect we then had of getting a chance to aid the boys."

Attention was increasingly focused on children who could not be sent to the reform school because they had not committed felonies. Judges continued to believe that it was important to remove these children from the influence of their "weak and criminal parents" and the "manifold temptations of the streets," so the children often ended up in poorhouses, police "lock-ups," or the county jail.

Julia Lathrop, who was later Chief of the Federal Children's Bureau, reported that in the six months prior to the establishment of the first juvenile court, 332 boys between the ages of 9 and 16 were sent to the city prison in Chicago.[7] Of that number, 320 were sent on a blanket charge of "disorderly conduct," which could represent a variety of offending behaviors from very trivial to fairly serious. About one-third of these were pardoned by the mayor, usually as a "favor" to the local alderman.

> But the significant fact which must not be overlooked is that, even if "let off" by the justice or pardoned by the mayor, no constructive work was done in the child's behalf. He was returned to the same surroundings that had promoted his delinquency, in all probability to be caught again and brought before another justice who, knowing nothing of the previous arrests, would discharge or find him again as seemed wise at the time. . . . Boys were kept in "lockups" and in jails in the company of adult prisoners, under circumstances which were a guaranty of ruined character, and were "let off with a scolding" by the justices because a jail sentence, however well deserved according to the law, was so manifestly bad for the boy.

From this quotation, it is apparent that officials in Chicago were confronted with the same dilemma that confronted officials in New York 75 years earlier: either punish harshly or do nothing. Both options seemed to increase crime among juveniles.

As a member of the Board of State Commissioners of Public Charities, Lathrop inspected all these facilities and raised a public outcry about the treatment of these children. Her report was presented in 1898, and contained arguments about preventing pauperism similar to those made earlier in New York:

> There are at the present moment in the State of Illinois, especially in the city of Chicago, thousands of children in need of active intervention for their

preservation from physical, mental and moral destruction. Such intervention is demanded, not only by sympathetic consideration for their well-being, but also in the name of the commonwealth, for the preservation of the State. If the child is the material out of which men and women are made, the neglected child is the material out of which paupers and criminals are made.[8]

Later that year, as a result of pressures generated by Lathrop and others, the annual meeting of the Illinois Conference of Charities voted to recommend the establishment of a separate court for juveniles. The idea was suggested by Frederick Wines, one of the most prominent penologists in the country, and quickly gathered wide support. It was passed unanimously by the Illinois Legislature on January 1, 1899, and went into effect six months later.

The Legal Model of the Original Juvenile Court

The legal problem that had been raised in the O'Connell case was the inability to deal with the "neglected child" who was "the material out of which paupers and criminals are made." The O'Connell decision ruled that such children could not be sent to reform school. In contrast, serious juvenile offenders were not a problem because they already could be sent there. If the new court was to be a solution to this legal problem, it had to get around the O'Connell ruling. A way to do this was found in the decision of the Mary Ann Crouse case.

In that case, the judge argued that it was legal to commit Mary Ann to the House of Refuge because of "parens patriae"—the fact that the state is the ultimate parent of all its citizens. The objection raised in the O'Connell case was that the state had no right to do this in criminal court. *Parens patriae* was a power in Chancery Court, which was a court in England to administer the property of orphans who had inherited estates. Legally, Chancery Court was supposed to preserve the best interests of the child until the child was old enough to take control of the estate. These courts had existed in England since the 1500s.

The solution to the dilemma therefore was to *define the new juvenile court as a chancery court, not as a criminal court.* This suited the purpose admirably. Chancery court was designed to help children who lacked proper parental care because their parents had died. But delinquent children lacked proper parental care because their parents were weak and criminal. Chancery court had nothing to do with punishment, but operated in the best interests of the children by conserving their estate. If the new juvenile court had nothing to do with punishment but only operated in the "best interests" of the child, then the legal objection raised in the O'Connell case would not apply.

Legal Steps to Establish the Juvenile Court

To establish a juvenile court as a chancery court required two separate steps: jurisdiction over juveniles had to be (1) removed from criminal court and (2) established in the new juvenile court. These two steps were contained in the legislation passed by the Illinois Legislature in 1899.

The first step was accomplished by raising the age of criminal liability to 16. Recall that under English Common Law, children under the age of 7 could not be convicted of a crime, no matter what they did, because it was held that they did not have sufficient reasoning ability to form a criminal intent.

The Illinois legislature raised this age to 16 in 1899, and eight years later raised it to 17 for boys and 18 for girls.[9] As a result, those who were younger than this age could not be charged with a crime in criminal court because legally they did not have sufficient reasoning ability to form criminal intent. This change in the age of criminal liability removed jurisdiction over juveniles from the criminal court.

Crime consists in *actus rea* (the behavior itself) and *mens rea* (the criminal intent).[10] If juveniles could not legally form *mens rea* and thus legally could not commit a crime, they still could kill people and force them to have sex, beat people up and break into houses, and knock old ladies down and take their purses. These would not be crimes, but they are "acts that would be a crime if committed by an adult." Similarly, people who are totally insane cannot commit crimes, but they can commit acts that would be a crime if committed by a sane person.

The jurisdiction of the juvenile court was defined in the Illinois law as including youth who violated "any law of this State or any City or Village ordinance."[11] That is, the new juvenile court had jurisdiction over any youth who committed an act that would be a crime if committed by an adult. This seemingly strange phrase remains in the language of the juvenile court today.

This accomplished the transfer of youths who had violated criminal laws from the criminal court to the new juvenile court. But criminal offenders were not the main problem—it was juveniles who had not committed any criminal offense but were in danger of growing up to be paupers and criminals. The new court must include jurisdiction over these youths or it would not solve the basic problem faced by these reformers. Thus, the Illinois legislature included the jurisdiction of the new juvenile court:

> any child who for any reason is destitute or homeless or abandoned; or dependent on the public for support; or has not proper parental care or guardianship; or who habitually begs or receives alms; or who is found living in any house of ill fame or with any vicious or disreputable person; or whose home, by reason of neglect, cruelty or depravity on the part of its parents, guardian or other person in whose care it may be, is an unfit place for such a child; and any child under the age of 8 years who is found peddling or selling any article or singing or playing any musical instrument upon the street or giving any public entertainment.[12]

It is difficult to imagine any poor child who would not fit under one or another of these provisions. In fact, this law was written so that the juvenile court could, if it wanted, take jurisdiction over every single poor child in the city of Chicago.

Of course, the authors of the law did not anticipate that all poor children would be brought under the court's jurisdiction. Rather, they wanted the court to take jurisdiction only when the child's best interests would be served. It was left to the court workers to make this decision. That is, this law provided court workers with virtually unlimited power over poor children, on the assumption that they would use that power for the good of the children themselves.

The new juvenile court, acting in its role as *parens patriae,* could take poor children out of their homes and place them in reform schools so that they would not grow up to become paupers and criminals. This practice was originally carried out under the Poor Laws, but their authority had eroded. Then it was implemented through the House of Refuge, but the O'Connell decision had undermined that legal basis. Now it was to be carried out through the new Juvenile Court. At last, there appeared to be a secure legal basis for this old and seemingly vital practice.[13]

Characteristics of the Original Juvenile Court

The Juvenile Court Compared to Criminal Court

The flavor of the new juvenile court can be sensed by comparing some terms in that court with those in the criminal court. The terms in the criminal court convey a sense of fault, blame, accusation, guilt, and punishment, while those in the juvenile court depict a sense of problems, needs, concern, helping, and caring.

TABLE 3. Comparison of Terms in Juvenile and Criminal Courts

Criminal court	*Juvenile court*
Indictment	Petition
Arraignment	Intake hearing
State v. *John Doe*	*In re John Doe*
Plead guilty or not guilty	Admit or deny offense
Trial	Adjudication
Pre-sentence investigation	Social history
Sentence proportionate to offense	Disposition in best interest of child

In criminal court, the process begins when the defendant is indicted. An indictment is a formal, written accusation that the person has committed a crime. In juvenile court, the process begins with a petition. A petition is a written request for something—a student might petition to get a grade changed, for example. The petition in juvenile court is a formal request for the court to look into the case of this particular child, to see if there is reason to take jurisdiction. The child is not accused of anything, only identified as possibly in need of help and attention.

In criminal court, the first phase of the trial process is the arraignment, where charges are formally read. The term arraign means to "call to account" or "accuse." In contrast, the first phase of the juvenile court is the intake hearing. "Intake" only indicates that a case is to be opened. The petition will allege certain facts that, if found to be true, would give the court the right to take jurisdiction over the child, but the child is not "called to account" or "accused" at this hearing.

The petition could allege that the juvenile committed an act that would be a crime if committed by an adult, or it could allege that the juvenile for some other reason is in danger of growing up to be poor and criminal. In the original Illinois law, this included that very lengthy list of facts: "any child who is destitute or homeless or abandoned; or dependent on the public for support, or has not proper parental care or guardianship; or who habitually begs, etc., etc." Later on, this portion of the law would be restricted to what we now call "status" offenses—mainly truancy, incorrigibility, and running away.

In criminal court, the case itself is named *"State* v. *John Doe."* That terminology implies a contest or fight between the state and the defendant, who must protect himself against the state. In juvenile court, the case name is typically *"In re John Doe."* This phrase means "In the matter of . . ." or "Concerning . . . ." There is no expression in the terminology that the state opposes John Doe or that John Doe must defend himself in any way.

In criminal court, defendants are asked at arraignment whether they are guilty or not guilty of the charges contained in the indictment. "Guilt" implies not only that the person committed the act (*actus rea*) but that they had criminal intent (*mens rea*). The juvenile court petition, in contrast, alleges that certain facts which, if true, would give the court the right to take jurisdiction over the child. The child is asked whether he or she admits or denies those alleged facts. In essence, juveniles are asked only about the *actus rea*—whether the alleged facts are true—but not whether they are "guilty"—that is, have criminal intent.

In criminal court, defendants who plead not guilty go to trial. The term trial originally meant to settle a dispute by a test or contest in which the two sides fight it out. Thus, at a criminal trial, the prosecution and defense fight it out. In juvenile court, a juvenile who denies the allegations receives an adjudication hearing. The term adjudication has the same root as the term judge. That is, at this hearing, a judgment is going to be made about whether these facts are true (as alleged in the petition) or false (as alleged by the juvenile). There is no implication in the term that the state is going to fight it out with the juvenile.

The outcome of a criminal trial is conviction, whose original meaning was to "overcome." A person who is convicted has been "overcome" in the trial in which prosecution and defense have fought it out. In juvenile court, however, the juvenile is adjudicated: that is, the judge formally states that the facts alleged in the petition are found to be true. The juvenile court therefore takes jurisdiction, which means that the court asserts the legal authority to decide what is in the juvenile's best interest.

Once an adult is convicted, the probation officer conducts a presentence investigation of the defendant in order to make a recommendation about the appropriate sentence. In juvenile court, the probation officer prepares a social history of the juvenile in order to recommend a disposition. The term disposition refers to putting things in order, or making a proper or orderly arrangement. Having declared the right to take jurisdiction over this youth, the judge therefore decides what will put the case in a proper order. Unlike the term sentence, a disposition contains no implication that the juvenile is to be punished, although that remains one of the options the judge has.

In criminal court, the sentence is supposed to be proportionate to the seriousness of the offense. In contrast, the disposition is supposed to be in the "best interests" of the child. This phrase was taken from Chancery Court, where it was used to describe the obligation to preserve the estate of the orphan. In juvenile court, it means every juvenile requires the love, care, and attention of a kindly (if firm) parent. When the child's natural parents could not or did not provide this, then the original Illinois law charged juvenile court to do so.

Juvenile Court and the Social Work Movement

Today, we usually think of the juvenile court as a version of the criminal court—kiddie court, perhaps. But originally, the juvenile court was not a criminal court at all. It was really a coercive casework agency. Casework is a term taken from the social work movement.

The social work movement was founded in Chicago about the same time as the juvenile court,[14] and some of the same people were involved in both.[15] The movement originally emphasized social reform: that is, it focused on changing the social conditions that gave rise to poverty and dependency. Social workers dealt primarily with the agents of the larger society such as city and state officials and leaders of the business community. The focus on social reform implied that the "blame" for poverty and dependency lay in the social conditions created and maintained by these powerful people, rather than in poor and dependent individuals themselves.

Social work soon shifted its focus from social reform to casework. That is, social workers stopped working with business and political leaders in order to change the urban environment, and began working with poor and dependent individuals to help them adapt to that environment. The focus on casework implied that the "blame" for poverty and dependency lay in the poor individual's failure to adapt, rather than in the urban environment itself. Casework became the primary focus of the social work movement.

The original emphasis on social reform was consistent with a view of the poor as "deserving"—that is, the poor deserved help and assistance because poverty and dependency were the result of larger social conditions, not their own failings and shortcomings. The later emphasis on casework, however, was consistent with a view of the poor as "paupers"—these people were thought to be poor because of their own failings and shortcomings, which therefore needed to be corrected. Because of their casework emphasis, most social workers in both England and America opposed financial aid to the poor since they believed it would only pauperize them further by making them dependent.[16]

The first law providing direct financial aid to poor children (now called Aid to Families with Dependent Children, or AFDC) was passed in Illinois in 1911 as an amendment to the Juvenile Court Act. Its purpose was to provide the court with an additional disposition for adjudicated juveniles:

> The Illinois Board of Charities, in arguing for the relief program, continuously stressed the causal connection between poverty (dependency) and delinquency. The juvenile court had available a variety of dispositions ranging from institutionalization to probation. The Funds to Parents Act amendment, in effect, gave the court another disposition. If the parents were "proper guardians" but "poor and unable to properly care" for the dependent child, then the court could grant aid.[17]

This law illustrates the continuing view that some poor people were "deserving" while others were "undeserving paupers." The "deserving" poor could receive direct financial aid to alleviate their poverty and help them raise their children in an appropriate way. The "undeserving" poor (i.e., paupers) would not receive this money since they presumably would squander it. Instead, their children would be taken from them by the state, acting as *parens patriae*, and they would be left to fend for themselves.

This law illustrates the close connection between the social work movement, a forerunner of our modern welfare system, and the original juvenile court. As originally conceived, the juvenile court was essentially a casework agency. That is, it helped individual children, especially poor children, adapt to their environment.

The Juvenile Court as Central Referral Unit

The juvenile court was to be the central referral agency for the entire child welfare system. The original founders of the juvenile court did not distinguish between children who committed crimes (whom we call delinquent children today) and children whose parents were unwilling or unable to provide adequate care and supervision for them (whom we call dependent or neglected children today).

In their view, it was the natural state of all children to be dependent. When children did not receive proper parental care and supervision, a variety of harmful effects could result, including crime and delinquency. But a child who committed a crime was not essentially different from a child who was merely neglected or dependent. The fact that a child had committed a crime was a minor point that had no real importance, other than supplying proof positive that the child lacked the proper parental care and supervision that all children, by their very natures, need.

Thus, all needy children, regardless of whether they had committed a crime or not, could be brought into juvenile court, where their "best interests" would be assessed and a recommendation would be made about the services needed to achieve them. The child would then receive needed services either from court workers or through a referral to people and agencies in the community.

Juvenile Court as a Coercive Casework Agency

The juvenile court was to be not only a casework agency, but it was also coercive. Other casework agencies were strictly voluntary: any individual who did not wish to be helped could simply refuse the services. But children whom the juvenile court wished to help could not refuse, any more than children could refuse services from their natural parents. The court, after all, acted as *parens patriae,* as the ultimate parent of the child. This positioned the juvenile court midway between casework agencies and the criminal courts.

TABLE 4. Juvenile Court as a Coercive Casework Agency

Casework agency	Juvenile court	Criminal court
Voluntary treatment	Coerced treatment	Coerced punishment

The idea of *coerced treatment* was the centerpiece of the original juvenile court. This idea was applied mainly to "salvageable offenders," such as Mary Ann Crouse and Daniel O'Connell, who had committed either status or minor criminal offenses. Juveniles who committed serious criminal offenses continued to be sent to the criminal courts.[18]

In that sense, the original juvenile court was an addition to, rather than a replacement for, the adult criminal courts. Juveniles who were "salvageable" could be sent to juvenile court first, where the attempt would be made to "salvage" them. If that attempt failed, then they could always be sent on to criminal court, where they would have gone anyway.

Legal Issues Concerning the Juvenile Court

The Case of Frank Fisher

Shortly after the Illinois law was passed, Pennsylvania established its own juvenile court. Frank Fisher was a 14-year-old boy who had been indicted for larceny in Philadelphia. His case was sent to this newly established court, from which he was sent to the same House of Refuge that had received Mary Ann Crouse sixty years earlier.[19]

Like Mary Ann's (and Daniel O'Connell's) father, Frank's father objected and filed a writ of *habeus corpus* in an attempt to get Frank released. Frank had been charged with (not convicted of) larceny, a criminal offense, so the "no punishment without a crime" issue raised in the Crouse and O'Connell cases did not apply. But a closely related principle was that, when a crime was committed, the punishment should be proportionate to the seriousness of the offense. Frank had committed a minor offense, but could be held in the House of Refuge until his 21st birthday, a total of seven years. This was much longer than he would have received in criminal court, and seemed disproportionate to the seriousness of his offense.

The case went to the Pennsylvania Supreme Court, which had also heard the Mary Ann Crouse case sixty years earlier. As it did before, it rejected the arguments of Frank Fisher's father. The argument that the court presented in announcing its decision contained all of the same essential points found in the earlier Crouse decision.

First, the court asserted that Frank was being *helped, not punished*, by being confined in the Philadelphia House of Refuge. Second, in making this assertion, the court focused on the *good intentions* of the state, especially in comparison to the poor *actual performance* of Frank's parents. Third, the court argued that helping Frank was legal because of the *parens patriae* powers of the state, now embodied in the juvenile court. Fourth, because Frank was being helped and not punished, the court held that he had no need for *due process protections:*

> To save a child from becoming a criminal, or from continuing in a career of crime, to end in maturer years in public punishment and disgrace, the Legislature surely may provide for the salvation of such a child, if its parents or guardian be unable or unwilling to do so, by bringing it into one of the course of the state without any process at all, for the purpose of subjecting it to the state's guardianship and protection. The natural parent needs no process to temporarily deprive his child of its liberty by confining it in his own home, to save it and to shield it from the consequences of persistence in a career of waywardness; nor is the state, when compelled, as *parens patriae,* to take the place of the father for the same purpose, required to adopt any process as a means of placing its hands upon the child to lead it into one of its courts.

Here we have a third legal case in which the decisions alternate between two separate lines of reasoning. The differences in the decisions do not arise out of differences in the facts of the cases—the facts of the three cases could be rotated and you would still get the same decisions out of these courts.

These decisions turn on whether or not the court was idealistic or realistic in its view of what was happening in the juvenile justice system.

TABLE 5. A Comparison of the Crouse, O'Connell, and Fisher Cases

	Crouse case and Fisher case	*O'Connell case*
Court focused on	Good intentions	Actual performance
Juveniles were said to be	Helped and treated	Punished
Legal basis of court's decision	Parens patriae	Criminal law
Decision	Due process is not required	Due process is required

The Crouse decision was handed down only thirteen years after the founding of the first juvenile institution. Hope still burned brightly for the wonderful good that would be accomplished in these marvelous institutions. But thirty years later, in the O'Connell case, those bright hopes for a solution to the problem of delinquency had faded in an increasingly ugly reality, and the court took a sober, realistic, even critical view of institutions.

The founding of the juvenile court infused new hope for the beauty of idealistic dreams. There was vast optimism that this new mechanism would soon solve the problem of delinquency. The Fisher decision, handed down only six years after the founding of the first juvenile court, returned to the logic and language of the Crouse decision.

Chapter 7 describes how, sixty years after the Fisher case, the Gault case would find its way to the United States Supreme Court. Its facts would be essentially similar to the facts in the three earlier cases, and all four sets of facts could be rotated among the different cases without influencing the decisions. But the passage of time would have dimmed the bright hopes for a solution to the problem of delinquency. The Supreme Court would therefore return to the language and logic of the O'Connell decision.

The Lessons of History

Why Did the Juvenile Court "Sell"?

The founders of the juvenile court proposed a new "idea" for juvenile delinquency: instead of a potential pauper, a juvenile delinquent was thought to be a dependent or neglected youth. This new idea of delinquency succeeded in the competition with other ideas and became the dominant interpretation of youthful offending for the next seventy years. Only recently has the popularity of this idea faded and other interpretations begun to compete with it.

Associated with this new idea of delinquency was a new idea of juvenile justice: the juvenile court. Like the juvenile institutions established seventy-five years earlier, the new juvenile court generated great optimism that it would solve the problem of urban property crime by lower-class youths. This, of course, did not happen. But the juvenile court succeeded in the sense that it triumphed over other possible policies for responding to this problem. By 1925, all but two states had juvenile courts, with the last state establishing its court in 1945.[20]

As in the last chapter, we can ask why these ideas were so appealing to so many people at the time. Phrased bluntly, we can ask why the new juvenile court and the new definition of juvenile delinquency "sold" so well. In answering this question, we have the perspective of ninety years of history to benefit us, so that we can get some distance to observe the larger shapes and patterns of events. In contrast, the reformers in Chicago at the time were immersed in their historical context and could see the trees clearly but not the forest.

The Cycle of Juvenile Justice

Like the problem faced by the reformers in New York in 1825, the problem faced by the reformers in Chicago in 1899 fits into the "cycle of juvenile justice." High juvenile crime rates were accompanied by a firm belief that these could be lowered by the proper policy response. Harsh punishments were available for juvenile offenders, but lenient treatments were not. Officials were often reluctant to impose harsh punishments, so many youths were simply released. Officials at the time, such as Julia Lathrop, thought that both choices increased juvenile crime.

The juvenile court, as a reform, was designed to provide leniency for those who would have been harshly punished by being sent to Chicago's jails and poorhouses, and to do something for juveniles for whom nothing would have been done by the adult criminal justice system. That is, it was designed to provide a middle ground between punishing harshly and doing nothing at all. In terms of "criminal justice thermodynamics,"[21] the juvenile court reduced the severity of the penalty to increase the frequency of its application.

The reformers in Chicago therefore were in exactly the same position that New York reformers had been in seventy-five years earlier. What had happened in those intervening years so that the juvenile justice system worked its way back to where it had started from?

There appears to have been a gradual evolution over the middle years of the 1800s, fueled by the belief that juvenile crime rates were unusually high and could be lowered by the proper policy response. The House of Refuge originally had been a "lenient" response that handled minor criminal offenders and status offenders. When it failed to solve the problem of delinquency, the natural response was to make it tougher. As it became tougher, justice officials naturally became reluctant to send minor criminal and status offenders to it, and increasingly sent serious criminal offenders who otherwise would have been sent to adult jails and penitentiaries. Many minor criminal and status offenders then were let off scot free because there were no lenient options available to do anything for them.

Thus, justice officials once again found that they had to choose between imposing harsh punishments or doing nothing at all. Juvenile crime rates remained high and now were attributed to the forced choice between two bad alternatives. A new reform—this time, the juvenile court—appeared on the scene to reintroduce leniency in order to solve this problem, and the cycle was ready to start over.

The Idea of Juvenile Delinquency: Dependent/Neglected Child

The original idea of juvenile delinquency proposed by the reformers in New York City was a slightly revised version of the old and popular idea that poor youths were "potential paupers." This idea remained popular throughout the 1800s, but it failed to reduce delinquency and so was vulnerable to attack by a new idea.

The new idea introduced by the founders of the juvenile court was that juvenile delinquents were dependent and neglected children. The natural state of all children was to be dependent and require the care and supervision of a kindly but firm parent. Children who lacked such care and supervision would exhibit a variety of problem behaviors, one of which was to engage in criminal and status offenses. But the participation in criminal offenses by itself did not mean that these children were different from other children who were dependent and neglected. Thus, dependency and neglect was the center of attention, rather than criminal behavior itself.

One reason that this new idea became so popular was probably that, like the earlier definition as potential pauper, it sounded new and different but it actually wasn't. Many forms of child protection legislation had been passed throughout the country since the middle of the 1800s,[22] and the social work movement became very prominent in the later part of that century. Thus, the concept of neglected and dependent children was widely known. It was really an older and well-established idea that was newly applied to juvenile offenders.

This new idea therefore did not require people to think anything different from what they had been thinking at the time. Fitting comfortably into the historical and philosophical context of the day, people got all the satisfactions of believing that they were taking an entirely new way of looking at things, but none of the trouble and inconvenience of actually grappling with new concepts and ideas.

The Idea of Juvenile Justice: Juvenile Court

The juvenile court as a method for responding to delinquents also seemed new and different and exciting and promising. Because it seemed so innovative, people were optimistic about how effective it would be in solving the problems of the day. In practice, however, the juvenile court returned to the practice of handling juvenile offenders that had been in effect before the O'Connell decision. Like the new idea of juvenile delinquency, the juvenile court was probably popular in part because it sounded new and different but it actually wasn't.

The juvenile court established a new legal basis for the old practice of sending poor urban children to rural institutions for their own good. Originally, the legal basis had been found in the poor laws, but that basis had eroded and was replaced by criminal laws in the Crouse decision. Even later, the O'Connell decision had found the criminal law basis inadequate, and the juvenile court established an even newer legal basis in *parens patriae* and Chancery Court. Thus, the practice survived and grew despite the fact that its legal basis kept disappearing.

Economic Interests of the Rich and Powerful

In the last chapter, I argued that the reformers who founded the House of Refuge had not tried to do anything about "the manifold temptations of the streets" other than remove children from them. From our perspective, it seems reasonable to conclude that the major problem was in the "streets"—that is, in the conditions under which poor children and their parents lived. Similar children and parents had lived in many other conditions in which no comparable problem of delinquency had appeared. Although it would have been possible to do something about these conditions, nothing was done and the idea was never seriously considered. The reason probably was that such actions would have threatened the economic interests of rich and powerful people.

Something similar seems to have happened with the juvenile court. The social work movement originally focused on social reform, but later changed that focus to casework. One can speculate that one of the reasons this transition took place was that efforts to reform society simply went nowhere. No one likes to beat their head against a wall. Eventually, social workers stopped trying to change the rich and powerful and started trying to change the poor and powerless. The seeds of both casework and social reform had been present at the beginning of the juvenile court, but only the seeds of casework sprouted and grew. The seeds of social reform withered and died.

Like the conditions in New York, it seems reasonable to speculate that the social conditions in Chicago were the principal cause of a wave of delinquency that engulfed the city. Dependency and neglect may have caused delinquency among some poor children, but it was not the main cause of delinquency among poor children at the time. The juvenile court triumphed in the competition with other possible policies precisely because it failed to address delinquency's principal cause—the social conditions under which poor people lived.

Moral and Intellectual Superiority of the Reformers

As with the reformers in New York City, there was great social distance between the small group of prominent and powerful people who ran Chicago and the large number of poor immigrants with whom they were concerned. These reformers chose an interpretation of delinquency that reinforced their own sense of moral and intellectual superiority. They believed that these children lacked proper parental care and supervision and therefore were "dependent and neglected." They also believed that, acting through the power of the state, they would be able to provide this proper care and supervision, although the children's natural parents could not.

With the perspective of ninety years of history, it seems reasonable to conclude that this probably was not the central problem. These poor parents probably were no more neglectful than poor parents had been at many other times and places where no comparable problem of delinquency appeared. What was it about that particular interpretation that led the reformers to adopt it, as opposed to other possible interpretations? In particular, why was this interpretation adopted over the original interpretation suggested by the social work movement: that the problem of delinquency originated in the social conditions in Chicago at the time?

I suggest that viewing delinquents as dependent and neglected children preserved the sense of moral and intellectual superiority of the reformers. This view would have been especially important for the women who founded the court, given their commitment to the traditional women's role as mother. By focusing on the inadequacies of these children's parents, these women were able to validate their own move out of their homes and into the larger society to use their talents and energies and abilities. In contrast, the social reform view too often implied that the source of the problem lay in the economic activities of their own husbands and fathers. Perhaps this view was too threatening to seriously consider for any length of time.

The "Unfair Comparison"

The "unfair comparison" likens an optimistic, idealistic assessment of the future, based on the good intentions of the reformers, with a pessimistic, cynical assessment of the past, based on actual performance of past policies. This comparison was found in both the Mary Ann Crouse and Daniel O'Connell cases, and fueled the earlier spread of the House of Refuge as a reform. This same type of comparison was used to promote the juvenile court as a reform.[23]

Viewed from our perspective, the founders of the first juvenile court made excessively optimistic appraisals of how effective this new organization would be in resolving the many problems of delinquency. In particular, they genuinely believed that the problem could be resolved in fairly short order by this new mechanism. That appraisal was based on an assumption that their own good intentions would be directly translated into actual practices. This, of course, was not to be.

At the same time, these reformers pessimistically viewed actual practices of the policies that existed before the establishment of the juvenile court. They focused on the dismal conditions in which juveniles were being held at the time, systematically ignored anything good about those practices, and systematically magnified anything that was bad about them. At no point was there any mention of the good intentions of those who had set up this system.

Once their own reforms had been implemented, however, these same reformers no longer focused on actual practices. Rather, in the face of increasingly awful conditions, they maintained their focus on their own good intentions, just as the original founders of the first juvenile institution. To do otherwise would have challenged their sense of moral and intellectual superiority. The road to hell may be paved with good intentions, but no one wants to believe that their own good intentions have produced hellish results.

Expansion of State Power

The actual procedures for processing juveniles did not change very much with the establishment of the juvenile court. The terms all changed, since the court was conceived as a coercive casework agency rather than a criminal court. But each new term was parallel to an old term in criminal court. In practice, the names changed but the game remained the same.

There was one important change brought by the establishment of the juvenile court—the power of the state to intervene in the lives of poor children was again expanded. The new juvenile court could take jurisdiction over virtually every poor child in the city of Chicago, as long as the case worker thought it was in the best interests of that child. It was no longer necessary for the child to have committed a criminal offense of any sort, much less a felony, for the court to send that child to an institution. The few due process protections that had been provided to juveniles were wiped out by the establishment of the new juvenile court.

Once again, an optimistic interpretation of the effectiveness of the new reform, based on the good intentions and moral and intellectual superiority of the reformers, was used to expand the state's power to intervene and to limit poor children's power to resist. Those protections were thought to be unnecessary because the state power would be used for the good of these children.

Generalizing the Lessons of History

The "lessons of history" derived here are quite similar to those derived in the last chapter from the story of the founding of the first juvenile institution in New York in 1825. These two events are sufficiently distant from us that we have some perspective on them: we can see the shapes and patterns of the forest rather than just the branches and leaves of individual trees. Gaining such perspective is harder in the remaining chapters of this book since those chapters concern events much closer to our own time.

Before we discuss more recent events, I want to "generalize" the lessons of history that I have derived so far. That is, I want to state them in a way that suggests they apply to more times and places than just New York in 1825 and Chicago in 1899. The question I will then consider is whether these lessons apply to events that occur in our own time.

Lesson 1: The Cycle of Juvenile Justice
High juvenile crime rates are accompanied by a belief that these rates can be lowered by appropriate juvenile justice policies. This results in a continuous cycle of reform. The cycle itself consists of establishing lenient treatments in a major reform, gradually "toughening up" those treatments over a long time so that officials end up choosing between harsh punishments and doing nothing at all, and then reestablishing lenient treatments in another major reform.

Lesson 2: Ideas of Juvenile Delinquency
Ideas of delinquency that "sell" (i.e., that succeed in the competition with other possible ideas) propose that delinquents are a subgroup within some larger problem group (e.g., paupers, dependent and neglected children) with which the public is already familiar.

Lesson 3: Ideas of Juvenile Justice
Responses to delinquency that "sell" (i.e., that succeed in the competition with other possible responses) are slightly modified versions of responses to the larger problem group of which delinquents are thought to be a subgroup.

Lesson 4: Economic Interests of the Rich and Powerful
Responses to delinquency that "sell" attempt to change the behavior of poor and powerless people but not the behavior of rich and powerful people. In particular, these responses do not harm the economic interests of the rich and powerful.

Lesson 5: Moral and Intellectual Superiority of Reformers
Responses to delinquency that "sell" imply that delinquents and their parents are morally and intellectually inferior, and that the reformers are morally and intellectually superior.

Lesson 6: The "Unfair Comparison"
Reformers "sell" their own reforms by an "unfair comparison" in which a harsh assessment of the actual practices of past policies is compared with an optimistic assessment of the new reform, based on their own good intentions. Because they assume that their good intentions directly translate into actual practice, reformers more or less promise to "solve" the problem of delinquency.

Lesson 7: The Power of the State
Reforms that "sell" increase the power of the state, based on the optimistic assessment of how effective the reform will be in "solving" the problem of delinquency, and on the (presumed) moral and intellectual superiority of the reformers.

Notes

1. See Harold Finestone, *Victims of Change*, Greenwood Press, Westport, 1976, pp. 38–42.

2. Charles Darwin, *On the Origin of the Species*, John Murray, London, 1859; and *Descent of Man*, John Murray, London, 1971.

3. See George B. Vold and Thomas J. Bernard, *Theoretical Criminology*, Oxford, New York, 1986.

4. For a contemporary example, see C. R. Henderson, "The Relation of Philanthropy to Social Order and Progress," in Frederic L. Faust and Paul J. Brantingham, *Juvenile Justice Philosophy*, West, St. Paul, 1979, pp. 48–58. This article was originally published in 1899 in Chicago.

5. Anthony Platt, *The Child Savers*, University of Chicago Press, Chicago, 1977.

6. Mennel, op. cit., p. 127.

7. Julia Lathrop, "Introduction," in Sophonisba P. Breckinridge and Edith Abbott, *The Delinquent Child and the Home*, Arno, New York, 1970, pp. 2–4 (original edition 1912).

8. Quoted in Mennel, op. cit., p. 129.

9. "Testimony of Judge Merritt W. Pinckney," in Breckinridge and Abbott, op. cit., p. 204.

10. See, for example, Joel Samaha, *Criminal Law*, West, St. Paul, 1983, Chapter 3.

11. Quoted in Mennel, op. cit., p. 130.

12. Ibid., p. 131.

13. See Platt, op. cit., p. 135; Sanford Fox, "Juvenile Justice Reform," *Stanford Law Review* 22:1187–1239 (June, 1970); and John Hagan and Jeffrey Leon, "Rediscovering Delinquency," *American Sociological Review* 42:587–98 (1982) for arguments that the

founding of the juvenile court codified existing practices rather than changed them.

14. Walter I. Trattner, *From Poor Law to Welfare State*, Free Press, New York, 1974, pp. 136ff.

15. Mennel, op. cit., pp. 151–52.

16. Joel F. Handler, *Reforming the Poor*, Basic, New York, 1972, pp. 6–10.

17. Ibid., p. 11.

18. Fox, op. cit.; Mennel, op. cit., p. 133.

19. 213 Pa. 48, 62 A. 198. The decision is reproduced in Faust and Brantingham, op. cit., pp. 156–62.

20. Mennel, op. cit., p. 132.

21. Samuel Walker, *Sense and Nonsense About Crime*, Brooks/Cole, Pacific Grove, CA, 1989, pp. 46–48. See pp. 36–37 above for a discussion of this concept.

22. Rendleman, op. cit.

23. E.g., see statements by Julian Mack and Merritt Pinckney, both of whom were juvenile court judges in Chicago, in Breckinridge and Abbott, op. cit. Mack's article is partially reprinted in Faust and Brantingham, op. cit., pp. 97–114. Breckinridge and Abbott founded the social work movement, and the book is introduced by Julia Lathrop.

7

Juvenile Justice Today— Good Intentions

By the 1950s, optimism about the juvenile court had broken down and a more realistic view began to emerge. This view was based on an assessment of the actual performance of the juvenile court rather than the good intentions of its founders. In practice, the juvenile court often did not "treat" juveniles or act in their "best interests," but only punished them for their offenses.

This new realism laid the basis for a reintroduction of due process protections: if juveniles are being punished, then they need at least some of the protections provided to adults in criminal court. That is, a shift began from the language and logic of the Mary Ann Crouse and Frank Fisher cases back to the language and logic of the Daniel O'Connell case.

By 1962, the two largest states, New York and California, had passed laws reflecting this new realism. These laws separated the handling of juveniles who had committed criminal offenses from those who had only committed status offenses, and provided some due process protections, including the right to be represented by a lawyer.[1] But the final return to the language and logic of the Daniel O'Connell case would be accomplished in the United States Supreme Court.

The U.S. Supreme Court and the Juvenile Court

In the 1960s, the United States Supreme Court issued a number of decisions that expanded the due process rights of criminal defendants in various areas of the criminal justice system. Some of these decisions concerned the juvenile justice system. There were five important decisions in nine years: *Kent* v. *United States* (1966), *In Re Gault* (1967), *In Re Winship* (1970), *McKeiver* v. *Pennsylvania* (1971), and *Breed* v. *Jones* (1975).

The Kent case was the first juvenile case ever heard by the United States Supreme Court. The Crouse and Fisher cases had gone to the Pennsylvania Supreme Court, while the O'Connell case had gone to the Illinois Supreme Court. The very fact that the Supreme Court accepted this case signaled its intention to apply constitutional protections to the juvenile process. By the time the *Breed* v. *Jones* decision appeared, juvenile had some (but not all) of the due process rights adults have in criminal court. The language and logic of the Crouse and Fisher cases were gone, and in their place was the language and logic of the O'Connell case.

Briefing Cases

In discussing these five cases, I use a modified version of the "legal brief." First the *facts* of the case are presented, which include both the crime that was committed and the process by which the case made its way to the United States Supreme Court. Second are the *issues* that the Supreme Court considered in the case. Third is the *decision* of the Court, and fourth are the *reasons* that the Court gave in reaching that decision. Fifth, I discuss any significant *dissent* to the opinion—that is, the reasons given by the judges who voted against the decision but were in the minority. Finally, I add some *comments* that put the case in its historic and political context.

The Case of Morris Kent[2]

Facts

In 1959, 14-year-old Morris A. Kent, Jr., was arrested and charged with several housebreakings and an attempted purse snatch. He was placed on probation and returned to the custody of his mother, who had been separated from his father since Morris was 2.

On September 2, 1961, while still on probation, Kent broke into a woman's apartment, raped her, and stole her wallet. He was arrested for this crime three days later and interrogated until 10 P.M. that night, during which time he apparently confessed to several such break-ins and rapes. He was also interrogated for all of the next day, when his mother retained a lawyer.

The lawyer quickly filed a motion for a hearing on whether to waive jurisdiction to criminal court, along with an affidavit from a psychiatrist asserting that Kent was "a victim of severe psychopathology" and recommending hospitalization. Given the seriousness of the offense, the lawyer assumed that the judge might want to waive jurisdiction, and he wanted the opportunity to argue against it. The lawyer also filed a motion to obtain the records that the probation office had kept on Kent for the last two years. He would use those records to support the argument that Kent should not be waived to adult court.

The judge received these motions but did not rule on them. He also received a new report from the probation department, dated September 8, that described Kent's "rapid deterioration of personality structure and the possibility of mental illness." The judge then entered a motion stating that "after full investigation, I do hereby waive" jurisdiction over the case, and ordered that Kent be held for trial in adult criminal court.

This precise phrase was important because the judge was required by the District of Columbia's Juvenile Court Act to conduct a "full investigation." However, the judge gave no indication of what that investigation was or why he had reached the decision to waive jurisdiction.

On September 25, about three weeks after the crime, Kent was indicted in (adult) criminal court on eight counts of housebreaking, robbery, and rape, and one additional count of housebreaking and robbery. The lawyer moved to dismiss the indictment on the grounds that the waiver from juvenile court had been invalid. In addition, the lawyer appealed the waiver itself to the Municipal Court of Appeal, and also filed a writ of *habeas corpus* demanding that the state justify Kent's detention.

The municipal court did not hand down its decision for a year and a half, until January 23, 1963. It rejected the appeal of the waiver and the writ of habeas corpus, and held that the only valid way to review a waiver decision was to move to dismiss the indictment in criminal court.

It then took up the question of whether to dismiss Kent's indictment.

The problem for the municipal court was that the juvenile court judge had given no indication of what investigation he had conducted or his reasons for the waiver. The municipal court decided it would not "go behind" the judge's statement that he had conducted a "full investigation." It therefore ruled that the waiver had been valid, and refused to dismiss the indictment.

For most of this time, Kent was in a hospital for the criminally insane, where he was diagnosed as schizophrenic. Following the municipal court decision, he was tried and found guilty by a jury on six counts of housebreaking and robbery. The judge sentenced him to five to 15 years on each count, for a total of 30 to 90 years in prison. The jury, however, found him not guilty on the rape charges on the grounds that he was insane. While this did not appear to be a very sane verdict, he was sent back to the same mental hospital. If that hospital ever decided his sanity was restored, he would be transferred to prison to complete the unexpired portion of his 30- to 90-year sentence.

Issues

Kent's lawyer argued that the District of Columbia statutes, especially the Juvenile Court Act, had been violated by the police and the judge in their handling of the case. In particular, he alleged that the judge had failed to make a "full investigation" before waiving Kent to criminal court. The lawyer also argued that the United States Constitution had been violated because Kent was denied various due process rights to which he would have been entitled if he were an adult.

Decision

The court decided the waiver violated the District of Columbia's Juvenile Court Act. Because it was based on District of Columbia statutes, the decision applied only to the District of Columbia.

The court ruled that Kent had been entitled to a waiver hearing, that he was entitled to have legal counsel at that hearing, that the hearing itself should have measured up to the essentials of due process, that the counsel should have had access to all records related to the juvenile, and that the judge should have made a statement of reasons for his decision. Finally, the Supreme Court issued a series of guidelines to consider in making a waiver decision, and ordered a new hearing be held to determine whether Kent's waiver had met those guidelines.

Reasons

Two decisions had been handed down by the Court of Appeals between Kent's crime and trial (1961 to 1963) and the Supreme Court decision in the case (1966). The *Watkins* decision in 1964 ruled that a juvenile's lawyer should have access to social service files in waiver cases, and the *Black* decision in 1965 held a juvenile was entitled to a lawyer in a waiver hearing. The Supreme Court affirmed these two lower court decisions and used relatively simple logic to extend them: if a juvenile is entitled to a lawyer at a waiver hearing and if the lawyer has the right to see the files in the case, then the juvenile must be entitled to the hearing itself, which Kent had not received.

In addition, the Municipal Court of Appeal had ruled that a waiver could be reviewed by moving to dismiss the indictment in criminal court. In this case there was nothing to review because the judge had not stated any reasons for the decision. The Supreme Court used relatively simple logic to extend this decision: since the waiver decision is reviewable, the judge must state in writing the reasons for the waiver so the review can be meaningful.

Comments

While this decision applied only to the District of Columbia, it had great national importance because of the general perspective the court took on the issues. Throughout the decision, numerous references occur to the need for due process protections in juvenile court.

For example, the court held the waiver hearing must "measure up to the essentials of due process and fair treatment." This perspective was a radical departure from the traditional juvenile court view that due process was unimportant because the "best interests" of the child were to be pursued. Stating the hearing must be "fair" suggests that the youth is being subjected to possible punishment.

But beyond that general perspective, the court actually described a specific line of reasoning for a future constitutional challenge to the juvenile court. In their view, this case raised a constitutional issue involving the equal protection clause of the Fourteenth Amendment. That clause says "no state may deny any person, under its government, equal protection of the law." In the past, the Supreme Court had interpreted this clause to mean people could receive "less protection" from the law only if they also received some "compensating benefit" that they could not obtain without sacrificing that protection. Juvenile courts provide juveniles with "less protection" than the criminal court provides adults, but juveniles were supposed to receive a "compensating benefit" in that the juvenile court looked after their "best interests," so that they were helped and not punished.

The Supreme Court questioned whether this "compensating benefit" really existed. Specifically, they stated that this case raised a "basic issue as to the justifiability of affording a juvenile less protection than is accorded to adults suspected of criminal offenses, particularly where, as here, there is an absence of any indication this denial of rights available to adults was offset, mitigated or explained by action of the government, as parens patriae, evidencing the special solicitude for juveniles commanded by the Juvenile Court Act."

In answering this question, the court indicated it would look at how juveniles were really treated in juvenile court, not merely at what the law "commanded." The focus was on the *actual performance* of the court, not just its *good intentions*. They went so far as to speculate that juveniles did not merely fail to receive special care and treatment, but that they actually received the "worst of both worlds":

> While there can be no doubt of the original laudable purpose of juvenile courts, studies and critiques in recent years raise serious questions as to whether actual performance measures well enough against theoretical purpose to make tolerable the immunity of the process from the reach of constitutional guaranties applicable to adults. There is much evidence that some juvenile courts, including that of the District of Columbia, lack the personnel, facilities and techniques to perform adequately as representatives of the State in a *parens patriae* capacity, at least with respect to children charged with law violation. There is evidence, in fact, that there may be grounds for concern that the child receives the worst of both worlds: that he gets neither the protections accorded to adults nor the solicitous care and regenerative treatment postulated for children.

The Court said "we do not pass upon these" constitutional questions because local statutes had been violated. Courts always rule on the narrowest possible grounds, so the court did not make a constitutional ruling in this case. But interested lawyers would interpret the above statements as an invitation to send the Supreme Court a case that did not violate local statutes but raised the same constitutional issues. That case came the following year.

Morris Kent himself got nothing out of this decision. Kent received a new hearing from the local criminal court on whether his waiver had conformed to the guidelines set forth in the Supreme Court decision. The criminal court found that it had. Kent was returned to the mental hospital, to be transferred to prison if he was ever found to be sane. Thus, the decision did him no good at all.

The decision had a major national impact, however. The decision applied only to the District of Columbia because it was based on local law, but courts across the nation adopted its guidelines on the assumption that a failure to do so would result in a successful appeal to the Supreme Court.

The decision also served notice that the United States Supreme Court would consider cases involving the juvenile justice system—after all, this was the first juvenile case they had ever heard. They also made it clear they would view the juvenile justice system from a due process perspective. *Parens patriae* was dead, and rising to take its place was the equal protection argument outlined in the Kent decision. A new juvenile court was being born.

The Case of Gerald Gault[3]

Facts

Gerald Gault, a 15-year-old boy who lived in Gila County, Arizona, had been on probation for about three months for being in the company of another boy who had stolen a wallet from a lady's purse. On June 8, 1964, he and his friend Ronald Lewis called their neighbor Mrs. Cook and asked her: "Do you give any?" "Are your cherries ripe today?" and "Do you have big bombers?"

Mrs. Cook called the sheriff, who arrested the boys and placed them in detention. When Gerald's mother came home at dinnertime she thought Gerald was over at the Lewis's and sent her older son to get him. But the Lewis's said that Gerald had been arrested.

The next day, Gerald's mother and brother went down to a hearing. No record was kept of this hearing, and Mrs. Cook did not appear. The judge later said Gerald admitted making the obscene remarks, whereas the Gaults said that Gerald only admitted dialing the phone. The judge said he would "think about it." Gerald was released from detention two or three days later.

A second hearing was held on June 15, with Gerald's mother and father both attending. No record was kept of the hearing and Mrs. Cook did not appear. Mrs. Gault asked that Mrs. Cook identify which boy made the remarks, but the judge said it was not necessary.

The judge then committed Gerald to the State Industrial School for Boys until his 21st birthday. That meant he could be held for up to six years, although he probably would be held between 6 and 18 months. If he had been an adult, the maximum penalty for this offense would have been a fine of $5 to $50 and imprisonment for not more than two months.

The Gaults then retained a lawyer, who filed a writ of *habeas corpus*, demanding that the state justify holding Gerald. This writ ultimately made its way to the United States Supreme Court.

Issues

In the lower courts, the lawyer argued that Gerald's treatment had violated both Arizona statutes and the United States Constitution. But in presenting the case to the United States Supreme Court, the lawyer narrowed the issue down to the denial of six specific constitutional rights in Gerald's adjudication hearing: the right to notice of the charges, the right to counsel, the right to confront and cross-examine witnesses, the privilege against self-incrimination, the right to a transcript of the proceedings, and the right to appellate review of the case.

Decision

The Supreme Court ruled that, in adjudication hearings that might result in being sent to an institution, juveniles had the right to adequate, written, and timely notice, the right to counsel, the right to confront and cross-examine witnesses, and the privilege against self-incrimination. Because the decision was based on the constitution, it applied to the entire nation, not just to Arizona.

The court did not rule on the right to a transcript and appellate review, although it encouraged states to provide those rights to juveniles. The court also did not rule on due process rights in other stages of the juvenile justice system, or in adjudication hearings that could not result in institutionalization (e.g., in some states juveniles cannot be sent to an institution for a status offense).

Reasons

The court first presented a general line of reasoning for why due process protections should be introduced into the juvenile court. It included all the arguments made in the O'Connell decision and also added the equal protection argument outlined in the Kent decision.

First, the Supreme Court concluded that Gerald was being *punished, not helped:*

> It is of no constitutional consequence—and of limited practical meaning—that the institution to which he is committed is called an Industrial School. The fact of the matter is that, however euphemistic the title, a "receiving home" or an "industrial school" for juveniles is an institution of confinement in which the child is incarcerated. . . . Instead of mother and father and sisters and brothers and friends and classmates, his world is peopled by guards, custodians, state employees, and "delinquents" confined with him for anything from waywardness to rape and homicide.

Second, the conclusion that he was being punished was based on an assessment of the *actual performance* of the juvenile justice system, not its *good intentions:*

> It is important, we think, that the claimed benefits of the juvenile process should be candidly appraised. Neither sentiment nor folklore should cause us to shut our eyes (to failures of the juvenile court).

Third, the court questioned and ultimately rejected the *parens patriae* doctrine:

> . . . its meaning is "murky and its historic credentials are of dubious relevance. . . . There is no trace of the doctrine in the history of criminal jurisprudence. . . . The constitutional and theoretical basis for this peculiar system is—to say the least—debatable.

Fourth, given a realistic appraisal of juvenile justice practices, the court concluded that there was a need for *due process protections:*

> The essential difference between Gerald's case and a normal criminal case is that the safeguards available to adults were discarded in Gerald's case. The

summary procedure as well as the long commitment was possible because Gerald was 15 years of age instead of over 18.

Thus, all four arguments that had appeared earlier in the O'Connell case reappeared in the Gault case. Added to these arguments was the equal protection argument that had been outlined in the Kent decision. Advocates of the juvenile court had maintained that juveniles were required to give up some of the law's protection in order to receive as compensating benefits the special care and concern afforded to juveniles. In contrast, the Supreme Court held that they could receive that special care and concern without giving up any of the law's protection:

> It is claimed that juveniles obtain benefits from the special procedures applicable to them which more than offset the disadvantages of denial of the substance of normal due process. As we shall discuss, the observance of due process standards, intelligently and not ruthlessly administered, will not compel the States to abandon or displace any of the substantive benefits of the juvenile process. . . . We do not mean to denigrate the juvenile court process or to suggest that there are not aspects of the juvenile system relating to offenders which are valuable. But the features of the juvenile system which its proponents have asserted are of unique benefit will not be impaired by (due process protections).

In this argument, the Supreme Court claims the benefits of the juvenile court are available *without* any reduction in the law's protection. Thus, no constitutional basis exists for providing less protection to juveniles than to adults. The Court went on to argue that due process itself offers an additional benefit:

> The appearance as well as the actuality of fairness, impartiality and order-liness—in short, the essentials of due process—may be a more impressive and more therapeutic attitude so far as the juvenile is concerned (than the informality of juvenile court).

The court then concluded the denial of due process to juveniles violates the equal protection clause:

> In view of this, it would be extraordinary if our Constitution did not require the procedural regularity and the exercise of care implied in the phrase "due process." Under our constitution, the condition of being a boy does not justify a kangaroo court . . .

Having completed its general line of reasoning, the Court made specific arguments about each of the six specific rights Gerald's attorney claimed he had been denied. It ruled that juveniles were entitled to the first four of those rights: right to notice, right to counsel, right to confront and cross-examine witnesses, and privilege against self-incrimination. In each case, the court emphasized how important these rights were for preparing an adequate defense. As originally conceived, of course, it was not necessary for juveniles to prepare a defense because juveniles did not have to defend themselves against a court that would act in their "best interests."

The Supreme Court did not rule on whether juveniles have a right to appellate review and to a transcript. These two issues are linked, since the transcript is only legally important when it is used as for appellate review. The Court pointed out that, although all states provide appellate review for adults, they are not required to do so by the constitution. Thus, they encouraged states to provide this for juveniles, but they did not require them to do so.

Dissent

An important "dissenting opinion" was written by Justice Stewart, who held on to at least some aspects of the language and logic of the Crouse and Fisher cases. Stewart implicitly accepted the *parens patriae* doctrine, describing juvenile courts as "public social agencies" rather than criminal courts. He focused on the good intentions of the juvenile court rather than its actual performance:

> Whether treating with a delinquent child, a neglected child, a defective child, or a dependent child, a juvenile proceeding's whole purpose and mission is the very opposite of the mission and purpose of a prosecution in a criminal court. The object of the one is correction of a condition. The object of the other is conviction and punishment for a criminal act.

Justice Stewart granted that the reality had not always lived up to this good intention, so that some juveniles may be punished rather than treated. But he argued that the intentions should be retained rather than rejected:

> There can be no denying that in many areas the performance of these agencies has fallen disappointingly short of the hopes and dreams of the courageous

pioneers who first conceived them. For a variety of reasons, the reality has sometimes not even approached the ideal. . . . But I am certain that the answer does not lie in the Court's opinion in this case, which serves to convert a juvenile proceeding into a criminal prosecution.

Finally, he granted the need for some modest infusions of due process, but not the wholesale injection that the court was granting:

> For example, I suppose all would agree that a brutally coerced confession could not constitutionally be considered in a juvenile court hearing. But it surely does not follow that the testimonial privilege against self-incrimination is applicable in all juvenile proceedings. Similarly, due process clearly requires timely notice of the purpose and scope of any proceedings affecting the relationship of parent and child. But it certainly does not follow that notice of a juvenile hearing must be framed with all the technical niceties of a criminal indictment.

This dissent contains the basic arguments, even if modified and restrained, of the Crouse and Fisher decisions. The court has good intentions even if actual practice has not measured up. It treats juveniles, and does not punish them. Thus, due process protections are not really needed, at least not to the extent the Supreme Court is granting them.

Comments

The Gault case is the fourth of an alternating series of cases that began in 1838 with Mary Ann Crouse. The crucial element of each decision is whether the Supreme Court focused on the *good intentions* or *actual performance* of the juvenile justice system.

If the Supreme Court focused on good intentions, then they ruled that juveniles are being helped and therefore do not need due process protections in juvenile court. If the Supreme Court focused on actual performance, then they ruled juveniles are being punished and therefore need due process protections just as adults need them in criminal court.

These alternating decisions were not the result of differences in the facts of the case. Rather, the facts in these four cases are sufficiently similar that they could be rotated and the decisions would remain the same.

Two lines of reasoning are available to the court, each legally sufficient. The courts alternate between these two lines of reasoning based on whether they are idealistic or cynical about the ability of the juvenile

TABLE 6. A Comparison of the Crouse, O'Connell, Fisher, and Gault Cases

	Crouse case and Fisher case	O'Connell case and Gault case
Court focused on	Good intentions	Actual performance
Juveniles were said to be	Helped and treated	Punished
Legal basis of court's decision	Parens patriae	Criminal law
Decision	Due process is not required	Due process is required

justice system to help children. The Crouse case came only thirteen years after the founding of the first juvenile institution, and the Supreme Court was still very optimistic about how well those institutions would work. The O'Connell case came thirty years later and the failure of the institutions was much more apparent. The vast optimism was renewed by the establishment of the first juvenile court in 1899. The Fisher case came only six years later, and reflected the firm belief that this new mechanism would work extremely well. Sixty years later, the Gault decision affirmed an awareness of the failures of that same mechanism.

The Case of Samuel Winship[4]

Facts

In 1967, 12-year-old Samuel Winship was charged with stealing $112 from a woman's pocketbook in a furniture store in the Bronx. A saleslady said she saw him dash from the store and then found the money missing. A defense witness, however, said the saleslady was in another part of the store at the time and could not have seen Winship. By New York State law, the judge was required to find a "preponderance of the evidence" in order to adjudicate. "Preponderance" meant that more evidence existed to indicate Winship did it than that he didn't. Winship was adjudicated delinquent and committed to a juvenile institution for an initial period of 18 months, subject to annual extensions for up to six years.

"Preponderance" is the standard used in civil courts because civil cases involve a conflict between two citizens—for example, the name of the case would be *"John Doe* v. *Jane Smith."* Using this standard, the judge decides which citizen is able to marshall more evidence. The judge then rules in favor of that citizen. "Preponderance" had always been the standard of evidence used in juvenile courts because they were considered civil, not criminal, courts.

In contrast, "beyond a reasonable doubt" is the standard used in criminal courts. "Beyond a reasonable doubt" is a much higher standard of evidence than "preponderance"—it means there is so much evidence of the person's guilt that there is no reasonable doubt left. This higher standard has been used in criminal court because the power of the state is arrayed against an individual citizen—the name of the case would be *"State* v. *John Doe."* The Founders of the United States were very concerned about abuses of power by the state, and were always seeking ways to limit that power. Thus, they set a very high standard that the state must meet before the judge can decide in the state's favor: the state must prove its case "beyond a reasonable doubt." In contrast, the standard for the defendant was quite low: if defendants can establish that there is a "reasonable doubt" about their guilt, then they are to be acquitted.

Winship's lawyer claimed to have established "reasonable doubt" about Winship's guilt by presenting a witness who said the saleslady was in another part of the store at the time. But the judge held that the preponderance of the evidence was that Winship had taken the $112. The lawyer got the judge to acknowledge this in the court record:

> COUNSEL: Your Honor is making a finding by the preponderance of the evidence.
>
> COURT: Well, it convinces me.
>
> COUNSEL: It's not beyond a reasonable doubt, Your Honor.
>
> COURT: That is true. . . . Our statute says a preponderance and a preponderance it is.

The lawyer then appealed this case all the way to the United States Supreme Court.

Issue

The legal issue in this case was "whether proof beyond a reasonable doubt is among the 'essentials of due process and fair treatment' required during the adjudicatory stage when a juvenile is charged with an act which would constitute a crime if committed by an adult."[5]

Decision

The "beyond a reasonable doubt" standard is required in adjudication proceedings in which the juvenile is charged with an act that would constitute a crime if committed by an adult. The "preponderance" standard may still be used in adjudication hearings that consider only status offenses.

Reasons

"Beyond a reasonable doubt" had never been held to be the constitutional standard in (adult) criminal court, although it was used in all such courts and was assumed in a number of earlier Supreme Court decisions. To remove any doubt about the standard, the Supreme Court first held "the Due Process Clause protects the accused against conviction except upon proof beyond a reasonable doubt of every fact necessary to constitute the crime with which he is charged."

The Supreme Court then turned to the use of the standard in juvenile court. They first considered the arguments of the New York Court of Appeals, which earlier had rejected Winship's claim. The New York Court of Appeals had argued that the juvenile court is designed "not to punish, but to save the child" and thus there is no need for due process protections; that the addition of due process protections would risk the destruction of the benefits now afforded to juveniles, and there is only a "tenuous difference" between the preponderance and the reasonable doubt standards.

In rather sarcastic language, the Supreme Court argued the first two of these arguments had been rejected in the Gault decision. It then called the "tenuous difference" argument "singularly unpersuasive" in light of the lengthy history of the reasonable doubt standard and the fact that the juvenile court judge had said on the record that there was a preponderance of the evidence but it was not beyond a reasonable doubt. This indicated a clear difference between the two standards, not merely a "tenuous" difference.

Dissent

Justice Stewart dissented from this opinion, as he had from the Gault decision. This time he was joined by the new Chief Justice Burger, who had been appointed by President Nixon to replace Chief Justice Warren.

Their dissent again contained the essence of the Crouse and Fisher arguments, focusing on the good intentions of the juvenile court while conceding that its actual practice had not always matched the ideal. They argued that due process protections were not required and would only make things worse:

> The original concept of the juvenile court system was to provide a benevolent and less formal means than criminal courts could provide for dealing with the special and often sensitive problems of youthful offenders. . . . I dissent from further straight-jacketing of an already overly restricted system. . . . My hope is that today's decision will not spell the end of a generously conceived program of compassionate treatment intended to mitigate the rigors and trauma of exposing youthful offenders to a traditional criminal court.

Comments

Two years later, the Supreme Court made the Winship decision fully retroactive.[6] This meant that youths who had been adjudicated on a preponderance of the evidence would either have to be released from institutions or readjudicated by evidence that was beyond a reasonable doubt. This was a very unusual step—normally, decisions only apply after they are announced.

This unusual move indicated how important the Winship decision was. The "beyond a reasonable doubt" standard is used to assure that when the court finds that someone has committed a criminal act, that finding is accurate. Adjudications based on a preponderance of the evidence were held to be not accurate enough to warrant continuing to keep someone in an institution. This same focus on accurate fact-finding reappears in the next case, where it involved the right to a jury trial.

The Case of Joseph McKeiver[7]

Facts

In 1968, 16-year-old Joseph McKeiver of Philadelphia was charged with robbery, larceny, and receiving stolen goods. These three felony charges arose from an incident in which McKeiver and twenty or thirty other youths chased three younger teenagers and took 25 cents from them. McKeiver had never been arrested, was doing well in school, and was gainfully employed, and the testimony of two of the three witnesses against him was described by the juvenile court judge as somewhat inconsistent and weak.

At the beginning of the hearing, McKeiver's lawyer said he had never met McKeiver before and was just interviewing him. The judge allowed five minutes for the interview. The lawyer then requested a jury trial, which was refused, and McKeiver was adjudicated and placed on probation.

The case was appealed to the Pennsylvania Supreme Court, where it was joined to another juvenile case in which a jury trial had been requested. Fifteen-year-old Edward Terry, also from Philadelphia, had hit a police officer with his fists and with a stick when the officer attempted to break up a fight Terry was watching. After denying a jury trial, the judge adjudicated Terry and committed him to an institution.

These two cases were appealed to the United States Supreme Court, where they were joined to two North Carolina cases that also involved juveniles requesting jury trials. Barbara Burris and about forty-five other black children between 11 and 15 years old had been arrested and charged with obstructing traffic as the result of a march protesting racial discrimination in the county schools. They had refused to get off the paved portion of a highway when told to do so by police. In a separate incident arising out of the same protest, James Howard and fifteen others created a disturbance in a principal's office. He was charged with being disorderly and defacing school property. The judge adjudicated all these youths and committed them to institutions. He then suspended the commitments and placed them on probation for terms ranging from 12 to 24 months.

Issue

"These cases present the narrow but precise issue whether the Due Process Clause of the Fourteenth Amendment assures the right to trial by jury in the adjudicative phase of a state juvenile court delinquency proceeding."

Decision

Jury trial is not required in juvenile adjudications.

Reasons

Unlike the New York Court of Appeals in the Winship case, the Pennsylvania Supreme Court presented a rationale for rejecting McKeiver's claim that incorporated a careful and thoughtful reading of the Gault and Winship decisions. The United States Supreme Court liked it so much that it relied heavily on it for its own decision.

The Pennsylvania Supreme Court argued that the United States Supreme Court had attempted to strike a balance that would preserve the benefits of the juvenile court while incorporating sufficient procedural regularity "to impress the juvenile with the gravity of the situation and the impartiality of the tribunal." They then argued (1) although faith in judges is no substitute for due process, juvenile court judges do try to handle cases differently than criminal court judges; (2) despite shortcomings, the rehabilitative facilities available to juvenile courts are superior to those available to criminal courts; (3) despite the fact that it is a punishment, adjudication of delinquency is less onerous than conviction of a crime; (4) despite its failures, current practices may contain "the seed from which a truly appropriate system can be brought forth"; and (5) of all the due process rights, jury trial is likely to be the one that would most disrupt and destroy the "unique nature of the juvenile process."

The United States Supreme Court agreed with this line of argument and expanded on it. The main function of jury trial in the original justice system is to limit possible abuses of state power, since conviction then requires the agreement of twelve ordinary citizens. The right to a jury trial therefore makes it hard for the state to use convictions as a political weapon. The Supreme Court held that this function was less important in the juvenile justice system than in the (adult) criminal justice system.

On the other hand, all the rights given in Gault and Winship had been designed to ensure accuracy in fact-finding during the adjudication hearing. Juries, however, have never been said to be more accurate in fact-finding than judges—if anything, research suggests that juries are less accurate. In addition, juries would be highly disruptive of the informal, cooperative atmosphere in which everyone tried to find the child's best interests, and would tend to create an adversarial atmosphere in which each side attempted to win the case. Thus, the Supreme Court held that juries were not required in juvenile adjudication hearings.

Dissent

A dissent was written by Justice Douglas, and joined by Justices Black and Marshall. These judges argued that juveniles were being punished, not helped, and therefore they were entitled to due process rights, including trial by jury:

> In the present cases imprisonment or confinement up to 10 years was possible for one child and each faced at least a possible five-year incarceration. No adult could be denied a jury trial in those circumstances.

They also argued that jury trial, like the earlier rights given juveniles, can contribute to the juveniles' sense that the proceedings are fair, which can help in the effort to rehabilitate. Finally, they argued that jury trials "provide the child with a safeguard against being prejudged by a judge who may well be prejudiced by reports already submitted to him by the police or caseworkers in the case."

Comments

The Kent and Gault decision had been written by Justice Fortas, who was one of the most liberal members of the liberal "Warren Court," headed by Chief Justice Warren. By the time of the McKeiver case, both Chief Justice Warren and Justice Fortas were gone, replaced by President Nixon's conservative appointments of the new Chief Justice Burger and Justice Blackman.

Justice Blackman wrote the McKeiver decision, and he was joined by Justice Stewart and Chief Justice Burger.[8] The argument in this decision is similar to Stewart's dissent to Gault and in Stewart's and Burger's dissent to Winship. Specifically, it focused on preserving the original good intentions of the juvenile court, despite conceding that actual practice had not always lived up to the ideal. Given this focus, the opinion opposed further "straightjacketing" of the system with due process rights.

One could argue the Supreme Court reversed itself in the McKeiver case: the dissenting opinions of Stewart and Burger in the Gault and Winship decisions became the majority opinion in the McKeiver decision. This change occurred because of the departure of liberals Fortas and Warren and their replacement by conservatives Burger and Blackman, who then joined Stewart in his opinion. This would be consistent with the fact that Justices Douglas and Marshall,[9] two of the remaining liberal members of the Warren Court, dissented from the opinion.

That is a possible interpretation, but it is also true that in many ways the McKeiver decision was consistent with and an extension of the Gault and Winship decisions. In the Kent decision, Justice Fortas accused the juvenile court of providing the "worst of both worlds," and in Gault, Fortas tried to preserve the benefits of the juvenile court while adding the benefits of the criminal court. That suggests he wanted the "best of both worlds," not merely to replace the juvenile court with a criminal court for juveniles.

The McKeiver decision, then, focused on preserving the "best" of the juvenile court world, whereas Gault and Winship had added the "best" of the criminal court world. In that sense, the McKeiver decision was consistent with, not a reversal of, the Gault and Winship decisions. The fifth and final case, written by Chief Justice Burger and joined by the new conservative majority, again focused on preserving the ideals of the original juvenile court.

The Case of Gary Jones[10]

Facts

On February 8, 1970, 17-year-old Gary Jones committed an armed robbery in Los Angeles with a loaded gun. He was arrested and placed in detention that same day. On March 1, Jones was adjudicated a delinquent on that charge, along with two other charges involving robberies with a loaded gun. The case was continued for two weeks so the probation officer could prepare a social history and recommend a disposition, and Jones was returned to detention.

On March 15, the court reconvened for the disposition hearing, but the judge announced instead he would waive jurisdiction to the criminal court. Jones' lawyer expressed surprise and requested a continuance in order to prepare arguments about the proposed waiver. The court continued the case for another week, then heard argument on the waiver issue and ordered Jones tried as an adult.

Jones' lawyer filed a writ of *habeas corpus* alleging Jones had already been "tried" in juvenile court for this offense, and could not be tried again in criminal court without violating the "double jeopardy" clause in the Fifth Amendment to the Constitution, which holds that no person shall "be subject for the same offense to be twice put in jeopardy of life or limb."

This petition was denied because the court held that a juvenile adjudication was not a criminal trial, so that Jones had not been placed in "jeopardy of life or limb" at it. Jones therefore was tried and convicted in criminal court and sentenced to prison.

Issue

The issue was "whether the prosecution of respondent as an adult, after Juvenile Court proceedings which resulted in a finding that respondent had violated a criminal statute and a subsequent finding that he was unfit for treatment as a juvenile" violated the "double jeopardy" clause of the United States Constitution.

Decision

With respect to "double jeopardy," juvenile adjudication is the same as a criminal trial. Someone who has been adjudicated in juvenile court for an offense cannot also be tried in adult court for the same offense.

Reasons

The "double jeopardy" clause states a person should not twice be placed at risk of punishment for the same offense. The question before the court therefore was whether the juvenile adjudication hearing constituted "jeopardy" in that the juvenile faced the risk of punishment for an offense.

Relying on arguments made in the Gault and Winship decisions, the Supreme Court said yes:

> We believe it is simply too late in the day to conclude, as did the District Court in this case, that a juvenile is not put in jeopardy at a proceeding whose object is to determine whether he has committed acts that violate a criminal law and whose potential consequences include both the stigma inherent in such a determination and the deprivation of liberty for many years.

They then stated the precise point at which jeopardy attaches, so the case can no longer be waived:

We therefore conclude that respondent was put in jeopardy at the adjudicatory hearing. Jeopardy attached when respondent was "put to trial before the trier of the facts," that is, when the Juvenile Court, as the trier of the facts, began to hear evidence.

The Supreme Court listed several reasons for selecting this point, but concluded with one that was consistent with their goal of trying to preserve the best of the original juvenile court while introducing some protections from criminal court. In the original juvenile court, the juvenile could be trusting and open with the judge because the disposition of the case would be made on the basis of the juvenile's "best interests." But a juvenile could not be trusting and open if the judge might turn around and waive jurisdiction to criminal court. The Supreme Court argued that the juvenile court judge's actions had placed Gary Jones in a dilemma that undermined the very trust that the original juvenile court tried to nurture.

If he appears uncooperative, he runs the risk of an adverse adjudication, as well as of an unfavorable dispositional recommendation. If, on the other hand, he is cooperative, he runs the risk of prejudicing his chances in adult court if transfer is ordered. We regard a procedure that results in such a dilemma as at odds with the goal that, to the extent fundamental fairness permits, adjudicatory hearings be informal and non-adversary. Knowledge of the risk of transfer after an adjudicatory hearing can only undermine the potential for informality and cooperation which was intended to be the hallmark of the juvenile-court system.

Comments

The *Breed* v. *Jones* decision was written by Chief Justice Burger and joined by all members of the court. From the point of view of the conservative members, this decision preserved aspects of the original juvenile court, while from the point of view of the liberals it added one more due process right to those granted in the Gault and Winship decisions.

This unanimous decision marked the end of the Supreme Court's restructuring of the juvenile court. It had begun in 1966 by the activist liberals on the Warren Court, but by 1975 the Supreme Court had itself been transformed by President Nixon's appointment of four conservative justices. Enough is enough, said the new conservative majority; it is time to preserve what was good about the original juvenile court, not just to change it even more.

The Lessons of History

The Supreme Court's reform does not seem consistent with the "lessons of history" derived from studying the earlier reforms in New York and Chicago and presented in the conclusion of Chapter 5. Consider each lesson in turn.

Lesson 1: The Cycle of Juvenile Justice
> High juvenile crime rates are accompanied by a belief that these rates can be lowered by appropriate juvenile justice policies. This results in a continuous cycle of reform. The cycle itself consists in establishing lenient treatments in a major reform, gradually "toughening up" those treatments over a long time so that officials end up choosing between harsh punishments and doing nothing at all, and then reestablishing lenient treatments in another major reform.

The Supreme Court's reform did not fit into this cycle because it neither established new lenient treatments in a major structural reform, nor gradually toughened up existing punishments over a long period of time. One would have expected that the next step in this cycle would have been the gradual toughening up of punishments, because juvenile justice officials were not yet confronted with a forced choice between harsh punishments and doing nothing at all. If Lesson 1 is correct, the Supreme Court's reform would have appeared strangely out of place, more or less irrelevant to general concerns about juvenile justice.

Lesson 2: Ideas of Juvenile Delinquency
> Ideas of delinquency that "sell" (i.e., that succeed in the competition with other possible ideas) propose that delinquents are a subgroup within some larger problem group (e.g., paupers, dependent and neglected children) with which the public is already familiar.

Lesson 3: Ideas of Juvenile Justice
> Responses to delinquency that "sell" (i.e., that succeed in the

competition with other possible responses) are slightly modified versions of responses to the larger problem group of which delinquents are thought to be a subgroup.

The Supreme Court proposed that juvenile delinquents were a subgroup of a larger group with which they were quite familiar: criminal defendants who were presumed innocent until proven guilty. Consequently, their response to delinquents was a slightly modified version of their response to this larger group: provide them with some (but not all) due process rights. This is consistent with Lessons 2 and 3.

On the other hand, the idea of criminals as defendants with rights never "sold" very well with the general public and lost most of its popularity once the "war on crime" escalated. To the extent that this broader idea failed to "sell," we would expect that the attempt to "sell" this idea with juvenile delinquents would also fail.

Lesson 4: Economic Interests of the Rich and Powerful
Responses to delinquency that "sell" attempt to change the behavior of poor and powerless people but not the behavior of rich and powerful people. In particular, these responses do not harm the economic interests of the rich and powerful.

The Supreme Court's reform did not attempt to change the behavior of the rich and powerful, but it possibly could have harmed their economic interests. A constitutional juvenile court would be more expensive, which could result in tax increases, and it would free large numbers of "guilty" juveniles who could then commit more crimes against wealthy and powerful people. These are relatively minor points, but it is clear that the Supreme Court's reform did not fall into the mainstream of what we would expect from this lesson.

A more important point is that the Supreme Court did not attempt to change the behavior of poor and powerless people at all. Instead, it attempted to change the behavior of juvenile justice officials. Again, this seems strangely out of place with respect to this lesson, more or less irrelevant to general concerns about juvenile delinquency. If this lesson is correct, then we would expect to find little public interest in the Supreme Court's reform.

Lesson 5: Moral and Intellectual Superiority of Reformers
Responses to delinquency that "sell" imply that delinquents

and their parents are morally and intellectually inferior, and
that the reformers are morally and intellectually superior.

The idea of juvenile delinquents as defendants with rights conveys the
image of a complete and whole person, not someone assumed to be
morally and intellectually inferior. In addition, by providing them with
due process rights, the court assumed that delinquents needed protection
from agents of the larger society, including the justices of the Supreme
Court itself. This implies that even Supreme Court Justices might not be
morally and intellectually superior. All of this contradicts Lesson 5.

Lesson 6: The "Unfair Comparison"
Reformers "sell" their own reforms by an "unfair comparison" in which a harsh assessment of the actual practices of
past policies is compared with an optimistic assessment of the
new reform, based on their own good intentions. Because they
assume that their good intentions directly translate into actual
practice, reformers more or less promise to "solve" the
problem of delinquency.

The Supreme Court criticized the actual performance of past policies
and generally promised a better situation in the future, but they did not
promise a "solution" to the problem of delinquency. They promised a
fair, reasonable, and constitutional method for responding to delinquents. Thus, their optimistic assessment of the future, based on their
own good intentions, did not promise what the public wanted: a solution
to the problem of delinquency. It seems unlikely that an optimistic
promise to deal with delinquents fairly would "sell" as well as an
optimistic promise to reduce or even eliminate delinquency.

Lesson 7: The Power of the State
Reforms that "sell" increase the power of the state, based on
the optimistic assessment of how effective the reform will be
in "solving" the problem of delinquency, and on the (presumed) moral and intellectual superiority of the reformers.

The Supreme Court's reform restricted the power of the state by
providing delinquents with the means for resisting the court's intervention. For the first time, the power of delinquents and their families was
expanded, and the power of those who work with delinquents was
limited. The Supreme Court took this stance because, like the Founders

of the United States government, they did not believe that government officials necessarily are morally and intellectually superior.

Conclusion

The Supreme Court's reform is inconsistent with each of the lessons of history learned from two earlier reforms. If those lessons are correct, then we can expect that this reform will fail to "sell," that it will fall by the wayside and become largely irrelevant in practice.

Beyond that, it seems likely that the Supreme Court's reform would be replaced by a reform that is consistent with the lessons of history. Such a reform would (1) continue the cycle of juvenile justice by gradually toughening punishments against juveniles and eliminating lenient options; (2) propose that delinquents are a subgroup within some broader problem group the public is already familiar with; (3) propose a method for responding to delinquents that is a modified version of the method for responding to that broader problem group; (4) positively attempt to change the behavior of poor and powerless people, but not the behavior of rich and powerful people or juvenile justice officials; (5) imply that delinquents are morally and intellectually inferior and that the reformers themselves are morally and intellectually superior; (6) optimistically promise a solution to the problem of delinquency, based on an unfair comparison between actual practices in the past and their own good intentions for the future; and (7) increase the power of the state to accomplish this noble task.

An alternate reform came into existence shortly after the Supreme Court's reform and met all these criteria. It was called the "get tough" movement.

Notes

1. Paul J. Brantingham, "Juvenile Justice Reform in California and New York in the Early 1960s," in Frederic Faust and Brantingham, *Juvenile Justice Philosophy,* 2nd ed., West, St. Paul, 1979, pp. 259–68.

2. 383 U.S. 541, 86 S.Ct. 1045, 16 L.Ed.2d 84; partially reprinted in Faust and Brantingham, op. cit., pp. 269–83.

3. 387 U.S. 1, 87 S.Ct. 1428, 18 L.Ed.2d 527; partially reprinted in Faust and Brantingham, op. cit., pp. 283–333.

4. 397 U.S. 358, 90 S.Ct. 1068, 25 L.Ed.2d 368; partially reprinted in Faust and Brantingham, op. cit., pp. 333–45.

5. Recall that juveniles cannot commit crimes *per se* because the law establishing the juvenile court raised the age of criminal liability. Thus, they can only commit acts "which would constitute a crime if committed by an adult."

6. *Ivan V. v. City of New York,* 407 U.S. 203, 92 S.Ct. 1951, 32 L.Ed.2d 659 (1972).

7. 403 U.S. 528, 91 S.Ct. 1976, 29 L.Ed.2d 647; partially reprinted in Faust and Brantingham, op. cit., pp. 345–68.

8. Justice White concurred in this opinion for a simpler reason that focused more strongly on the intention of the juvenile court to help, not punish, juveniles. Justice Harlan concurred in the decision but for a different reason. He argued that jury trials are not constitutionally required in adult criminal courts, so they are not required in juvenile courts either.

9. Justice Brennan, another liberal member of the court, dissented in the North Carolina cases, but concurred in the Pennsylvania cases. In his view, jury trial was not required if the public and press were admitted to adjudication hearings, as was the case in Pennsylvania.

10. 421 U.S. 519, 95 S.Ct. 1779, 44 L.Ed. 2d 346; partially reprinted in Faust and Brantingham, op. cit., pp. 368–81.

8

Juvenile Justice Today— Actual Practice

The new constitutional juvenile court was supposed to have the "best of both worlds": due process protections in the adjudication hearing along with care and treatment in the disposition hearing. But this smooth blending of two worlds was not to be.[1]

The "best" of the criminal court was due process protections in the adjudication hearing. But for various practical reasons, adjudication hearings are rarely held. In the few that take place, judges are free to ignore or "bend" due process requirements because there is no right to a jury trial and because appeal of a juvenile court adjudication is almost non-existent. Thus, in practice, juveniles did not receive the "best" of the criminal court.

The "best" of the original juvenile court was care and treatment in the disposition hearing. But the Supreme Court pointed out that juveniles did not actually receive this care and treatment before the Gault decision because of a lack of financial resources. While they claimed to preserve this "best" aspect of the juvenile court in their decision, the Supreme Court did nothing to ensure that juveniles would actually receive it. In practice, juveniles did not receive any more treatment after the Gault decision than they had before it.

The Supreme Court had good intentions in issuing their constitutional rulings, but in actual practice, juveniles did not receive either due process protections in adjudication hearings or care and treatment in disposition hearings. If the juvenile court really contained the "worst of both worlds" before the Gault decision, then it contained the same thing after it.

This is a harsh assessment of the impact of the Supreme Court's decisions. In order to demonstrate that this assessment is correct, I discuss the types of changes that would have appeared in juvenile court had the Supreme Court decisions been effective in practice. I then argue that these changes simply did not occur. We begin with changes in the adjudication hearing.

Did the Adjudication Hearing Change in Actual Practice?

The Central Issue: Discretion vs. Due Process

The central issue in the Supreme Court decisions was whether the adjudication hearing would be characterized by discretion or due process. Both ways have advantages and disadvantages, but you cannot do both at the same time.

In the original juvenile court, officials had a great deal of discretion. The hearing was very flexible and informal, and few standards or procedures had to be followed. This allowed intelligent, competent, and well-motivated officials to help kids, which of course was a good idea. The problem was that it also allowed stupid, incompetent, and evil officials to hurt kids.

To solve this problem, the Supreme Court imposed due process protections on the adjudication hearing. These were set standards and procedures that must be followed in every case, so that the hearings no longer were flexible and informal. As a result, stupid, incompetent, evil, or simply fallible officials no longer were able to hurt kids as easily. The problem was that intelligent, competent, and well-motivated officials no longer were able to help as easily.

The conflict between due process and discretion presents a dilemma for public policy. Each position has benefits, but each also has costs. Neither position is perfect.

The Case for Discretion

Most people in the juvenile justice system are intelligent, competent, and well-motivated. They try to do what is best for the child and they often succeed. Like everyone else, they make mistakes. But on the whole, most juvenile justice officials do a good job working in difficult situations.

Because the problems they deal with often are very complex, it can be argued that juvenile justice officials need flexibility in their jobs. They need to have the freedom to respond to different cases differently, so that they can help as many children as much as possible. That is, they need discretion.

This was the point of view of the original founders of the juvenile court: they thought due process protections interfered with the ability of juvenile justice officials to help children. Chief Justice Burger took the same stance in his dissent to the Winship decision, saying that due process protections amount to "strait-jacketing of an already overly restricted system":

> What the juvenile court system needs is not more but less of the trappings of legal procedure and judicial formalism; the juvenile court system requires breathing room and flexibility in order to survive. . . .

The Case for Due Process

Two hundred years ago, the Founders of the United States government were faced with the same choice between discretion and due process. They decided in favor of due process. Having just rebelled against what they believed was a tyrannical government, they did not trust the good intentions of government officials, and created a government based on separation of powers and a system of checks and balances. This system was designed to restrict and restrain the power of the state in almost every area. The Founders knew that restricting state power would cause many problems, but they believed that the costs were worth the benefits of a society protected from tyranny.

In criminal court, the Founders restrained the power of the state by providing defendants with due process rights. The state's power to convict defendants was severely limited. The Founders knew this would cause many problems—under such a system, many guilty defendants surely would be freed. But the Founders believed that the costs were worth the larger benefits of a system where the state could not easily convict anyone it wanted. Tyrants have always used criminal courts to convict their enemies.

Today, due process rights are sometimes criticized for "handcuffing" the police, but the intent of the Founders of the United States was to do precisely that. The Founders believed that in the long run the country would be better served by a justice system that had to obey strict rules of fairness, even if it freed many guilty criminals. A saying expressed this position: "Better a hundred guilty people go free than one innocent person be convicted."

These same considerations motivated the Supreme Court to give due process rights to juveniles. The guiding thread of reasoning through all the Supreme Court decisions was that the juvenile had to be given sufficient due process rights to ensure accuracy of fact-finding in the adjudication hearing. This reasoning was most apparent in the Winship decision, which required that the state prove its case "beyond a reasonable doubt."

Like the Founders of the United States two hundred years ago, the Supreme Court knew that many "guilty" juveniles would be freed by their decision. For example, they made the Winship decision retroactive, which freed from institutions many juveniles who had committed serious offenses. But the Supreme Court believed that this was better than adjudicating a few juveniles who had not actually committed the offense. Despite the costs associated with this position, the court felt that history demonstrated that the Founders of the United States had made the right choice:

> Juvenile court history has again demonstrated that unbridled discretion, however benevolently motivated, is frequently a poor substitute for principle and procedure.

Expected Change in Adjudication Hearings

The good intentions of the Supreme Court were to add due process protections to the adjudication hearing. If these intentions were translated into actual practice, then we would expect to find changes in the number of "innocent" juveniles adjudicated and the number of "guilty" juveniles released.

Before the Supreme Court decisions, juveniles had no due process rights and thus were unable to protect themselves against the power of the state, even if that power was "benevolently motivated." This was consistent with the position taken by the founders of the first juvenile institution and the first juvenile court. They simply were not very concerned about whether the juveniles they "helped" had committed an offense. For example, Thomas Eddy, one of the founders of the first institution, argued that juveniles who had not committed any offense should be sent to the House of Refuge in order to prevent their entry into a life of crime.

After the Supreme Court decisions, juveniles would have the power to fight against the state. The intent was to prevent the adjudication of "innocent" juveniles, but the cost was that many "guilty" juveniles also would be freed. This would be consistent with the position taken by the Founders of the United States Government: better one hundred "guilty" juveniles be freed than even one "innocent" juvenile be adjudicated.

To sum it up, before the Supreme Court decisions, we would expect to find *more* "innocent" juveniles who were adjudicated and *fewer* "guilty" juveniles who were released. After the Supreme Court decisions, we would expect *fewer* "innocent" juveniles who are adjudicated, and *more* "guilty" juveniles who are released. Now let us look at adjudication hearings before and after the Supreme Court decisions to see if these changes actually have occurred.

Pre-Gault Adjudication Hearings

Justice Fortas described the juvenile court that adjudicated Gerald Gault as "a kangaroo court." While the term seems appropriate for what happened to Gault, most youths processed by juvenile courts did not receive such outrageous treatment before the Gault decision. Most juveniles were treated fairly and reasonably, with court officials trying to promote the child's best interests as much as possible. "Kangaroo" juvenile courts were the exception, not the rule, in the pre-Gault era.[2]

Even if most juvenile courts were fair and reasonable, there were no legal barriers to running a "kangaroo court" if that is what court officials wanted to do. Under existing juvenile court laws, juvenile court officials had the discretion to do almost anything they wanted. The juvenile had no due process rights to be treated according to set standards of fairness. Most courts acted according to such standards because they thought it was best to do so.

Nevertheless, some looseness about the procedure occurred in the pre-Gault era. There was more focus on the needs of the child, and more certainty that the actions of the court would meet those needs. Because court officials thought of themselves as on the side of the child, there was less concern about proving that the child had actually committed an offense. The juvenile court was closer to its heritage as a coercive casework agency, and court workers did not think of themselves as working in a criminal court that punished offenders. The criminal court concepts were there, but were less central to the identity of the agency, a marginal aspect of what the court was all about.

The "looseness" in the adjudication hearing meant that few "guilty" juveniles were freed while relatively many juveniles who were otherwise innocent were adjudicated. Consider, for example, the cases that reached the United States Supreme Court, as described in Chapter 6. These were not unusual cases in terms of the way they were handled. No formal evidence was taken against Gerry Gault, and it was not clear that he had actually committed the offense. There was "reasonable doubt" about whether Winship really had stolen that money. The evidence against McKeiver was described as "weak and inconsistent," and in the North Carolina cases that were joined to McKeiver, the juvenile court was essentially used to suppress the civil rights movement. Only the cases against Morris Kent and Gary Jones seemed solid enough to warrant conviction in criminal court, and both of them in fact were waived to criminal court.

The point is that, in the juvenile court, judges often were not excessively concerned with whether the juvenile really committed the offense. Rather, they often looked at the case in terms of whether the juvenile needed help. If so, they would take jurisdiction and see what help could be provided.

There seems little doubt that, before the Supreme Court decisions, relatively few "guilty" juveniles were freed while relatively many "innocent" juveniles were adjudicated in order to be given the help they needed. Now let us see if the situation changed after the Supreme Court decisions.

Post-Gault Adjudication Hearings

The Supreme Court decisions generally resulted in some shift in this "loose" attitude. Juvenile court officials now are more aware that their court has many elements of a criminal court, that juveniles are punished by the court even if such punishment is in their best interests, that juveniles deserve to have legal rights and protections to ensure that they are treated fairly. Many of the freewheeling practices of the past are gone.

Nevertheless, this change is not nearly as broad as the Supreme Court thought it would be. Court workers continue to think in terms of helping, not punishing juveniles. When due process protections prevent them from providing that help, they may bend the rules a bit to be able to do it. After all, the court official might say, it is in the child's best interests for the court to take jurisdiction. And often the official is right: bending the rules is in the child's best interests.

Bending the rules means that, in actual practice, juvenile officials still have a great deal of discretion despite the Supreme Court's decisions. There are a variety of reasons for this, which are discussed in detail below. To give a brief overview, most of the juvenile's due process rights are in the adjudication hearing, but few of these hearings are ever held because almost all juveniles admit the offense they are charged with. When an adjudication hearing is held, judges can adjudicate when there is reasonable doubt, even though they are required by law to have evidence "beyond a reasonable doubt." They are able to do that because juveniles have no right to a jury trial and because, for a variety of practical reasons, appeals of a juvenile adjudication are virtually non-existent.

Why Are There So Few Adjudication Hearings?

Although most youths referred to juvenile court are adjudicated, fewer than 5% of cases referred to juvenile courts result in an adjudication hearing.[3] The reason is that although juveniles have a privilege against self-incrimination, the vast majority of them admit the offense with which they are charged.[4] Much more than adults, they are influenced by criminal justice officials who urge them to tell the truth. In the face of police questioning, one study found that fewer than 10% of juveniles asserted their right to remain silent, and that assertion of this right was virtually non-existent among youths below the age of 15.[5]

To counterbalance this tendency, juveniles may only be questioned in the presence of an "interested adult," preferably the parent.[6] It is presumed that this adult will take care that the juvenile's rights are protected. But the above study found that only 20% of parents agreed that their children had the right to withhold information from the police or courts.[7] More often, these "interested adults" were interested in having the juvenile admit the offense. Parents often are very angry at a juvenile who gets into trouble with the law. They throw up their hands and tell the officials to put the kid in an institution.

The privilege against self-incrimination was one of the five due process protections granted in the Gault and Winship decisions, but it is largely inoperative in practice. Once the child has admitted the offense, then there is no occasion to exercise the other four rights in the adjudication hearing: notice, counsel, confront and cross-examine witnesses, and evidence that is beyond a reasonable doubt.

Why Do Almost All Adjudication Hearings Find That the Youth Committed the Offense?

Adjudication hearings are held on those relatively few occasions when the juvenile denies the alleged offense, but the outcome of these hearings is almost always that the juvenile is found to have committed the offense.[8] In one juvenile court, for example, the public defender stated:

> Adjudication has become a farce here, especially in the judge's chambers. . . . He doesn't need to find a child guilty of a major offense. He only wants some legal basis upon which to act. My role is almost nothing. Now I'm more into dispositional matters.[9]

Carey and McAnany comment that the few adjudications that occur

> take place on a "show" basis, to convince the juvenile and the juvenile's family that he or she is getting justice, and to placate the instincts of the lawyers involved that they are doing justice. This sense of "show justice" might even be rationalized by defense counsel as necessary . . . to get the juvenile into the right frame of mind for help. Though there is no research that demonstrates this hypothesis, there are anecdotal references and evidence from the low rate of successful outcomes (acquittals) that may suggest it.[10]

The lack of research to demonstrate this hypothesis stems from the fact that no separate reporting category in juvenile court statistics is kept for juveniles who are "acquitted"—that is, when the court finds that the juvenile did not commit the offense. That seems remarkable, but is explained by the fact that, in actual practice, a referral to the court almost always leads to the conclusion that the juvenile committed the alleged act.

The court can release the youth without any punishment—this is the outcome in approximately 42% of delinquency cases referred to juvenile courts.[11] But release does not indicate a finding that the youth did not commit the offense. Rather, release is normally a disposition, like probation or institutionalization. It is assumed that the juvenile actually committed the offense and is being given a "break" for one reason or another. If the youth later returns to court, it is assumed that the youth did not "learn a lesson" from getting this break, so will get harsher treatment the next time.

In some courts, the certainty of adjudication is so great that probation officers prepare the "social history" (a rather lengthy and time-consuming document) before the adjudication hearing. They can then hold the disposition hearing immediately after the adjudication instead of waiting several weeks for the document to be completed. This is a more efficient procedure, of course, but if the judge found the juvenile did not commit the offense, then all that work would be for nothing. One would think that probation officers would be reluctant to do these reports until after the adjudication. Yet in practice, adjudication is a foregone conclusion and the probation officer risks nothing by completing the social history ahead of time.

The reason for the high certainty of adjudication ultimately lies in the fact that the juveniles have no right to a jury trial. In adult courts, having a trial before a judge (as opposed to a jury) is sometimes described as a "slow plea of guilty."[12] The phrase suggests that, rather than go through a trial before a judge, the defendant should simply plead guilty and get it over with. Many defense attorneys therefore enter a "not guilty" plea only if they also request a jury trial.

But juveniles have no right to jury trials because of the McKeiver decision. Defense lawyers (realistically) may advise their juvenile clients to admit the offense even if the juveniles claim they did not commit it, because the judge is going to find that they committed it anyway.

In essence, juvenile court judges are free to adjudicate on evidence that does not meet the "beyond a reasonable doubt" standard.[13] They do this when they decide (correctly, in most cases) that the juvenile probably did it and when they are going to be concerned about the juvenile's best interests in the disposition hearing. When judges do not intend to punish the juvenile but provide care and treatment, proof beyond a reasonable doubt can seem somewhat irrelevant.

In practice, the McKeiver decision (no right to a jury trial) means that juvenile court judges can ignore the Winship decision and adjudicate when there is only a "preponderance" of the evidence. Many juvenile court judges do this because their intent is to help (not punish) the juvenile, who clearly needs help and who probably committed the offense anyway.

Why Are There So Few Appeals?

Almost all juveniles referred to a juvenile court are found to have committed the offense they were charged with. Most admit the offense, and almost all of the rest are found in an adjudication hearing to have committed the offense. Very few juveniles referred to a juvenile court are found to be "innocent."

But no system can be perfect. There must be at least some juveniles referred to the juvenile court who did not commit their offenses. It may be hard to figure out which ones they are, but there is no question that some "innocent" juveniles exist. Most of them will be found to have committed the offense. Why would they not appeal their cases to a higher court?

The Gault decisions did not give juveniles the right to appeal, but most states provide some mechanism for appeal anyway.[14] For various practical reasons, appeals from juvenile adjudications are virtually nonexistent.

First, juvenile defense lawyers typically have an extremely heavy workload which simply does not permit the luxury of appealing cases. For example, when Patrick Murphy took over the Juvenile Office of the Legal Aid Society of Chicago in 1970, the first thing he did was to cut workload to one-third of its former level.[15] This was difficult to do personally because it meant turning away so many cases of children who really needed defense lawyers in court. It was also difficult to do professionally because other people in the juvenile court organization objected to his failure to represent juveniles in court. But Murphy wanted to focus on appeals, which are quite time consuming, and to do that he had to reduce the number of court cases. Many juvenile defense lawyers are unwilling to take such a drastic step.

Second, there often is less at stake in a juvenile appeal than in an adult appeal. Juveniles frequently are placed on probation, or if they are sent to an institution, they usually get out in six to eighteen months. Appeals can take years, and the juvenile often has been released long before the appeal is settled.

Third, there is organizational pressure against appealing a case be-cause of the treatment orientation of the court. Other court officials more or less say: Look, we are all acting in this kid's best interests, so why are you messing up the works?

Fourth, juvenile justice officials can retaliate against the kids involved in the appeal. In many cases that Murphy appealed, the juveniles in the case were held in institutions for as long as the appeal was alive, whereas they would have been released much earlier if no appeal had been filed. Some were even repeatedly placed in solitary confinement, apparently because they were seen as "troublemakers." Defense lawyers who care about kids are often reluctant to expose them to this risk of retaliation.

Fifth, given the informality of juvenile court proceedings, much of what is at issue in an appeal is not on any written record and therefore cannot be considered in an appeal anyway.

Sixth, most states provide a mechanism for juvenile appeals but they do not provide transcripts, which can be quite costly. In addition, there is no right to counsel on appeal. A youth who has the funds to purchase a transcript and hire a lawyer for the appeal probably had the funds to hire a private lawyer for the original adjudication hearing and therefore does not need to appeal the case.

Conclusion

If due process rights influence adjudication hearings in actual practice, we would expect to find fewer "innocent" juveniles who are adjudicated and more "guilty" juveniles who are acquitted. Instead, we find that virtually all juveniles are found to have committed the offense with which they were charged. Most admit the offense, and most of the rest are found to have committed the offense in an adjudication hearing. A substantial portion of youths are released without punishment, but this is treated as a disposition, evidence of the court's lenient handling of young offenders. Few youths are found to be "innocent" in the sense of not committing the offense they were charged with.

This is the opposite of what we would expect in a court that was governed by due process protections. The due process protections imposed on the juvenile court by the Supreme Court therefore do not determine its actual practice. The lack of a right to a jury trial and unavailability of appeal underlies this situation.

This situation has benefits: intelligent, competent and well-intentioned court officials remain free to help children whom they might otherwise have been unable to help. It also has costs: stupid, incompetent, and evil court officials remain free to harm children whom they otherwise would have been prevented from harming. Despite the Supreme Court decisions, nothing really changed in actual practice. Officials still have almost total discretion in determining which youths they want to "help," and juveniles and their parents still have little power to resist that "help."

Did the Disposition Hearing Change in Actual Practice?

Expected Changes in Disposition Hearings

Juveniles receive less protection from the law because they do not have all the due process rights of adults. The Supreme Court held that this did not violate the "equal protection" clause of the constitution because the juvenile court provides juveniles with a compensating benefit: a juvenile receives care and treatment from juvenile court, whereas an adult receives punishment from criminal court.[16]

The provision of care and treatment therefore is essential to the Court's constitutional argument. It is also essential to the Court's new conception of the juvenile court: "the best of both worlds." Care and treatment in the disposition hearing were the "best" of the original juvenile court, and so it is one-half of the "best of both worlds" that the Supreme Court proposed as their new conception of the juvenile court.

Despite its importance for their constitutional argument and for their new conception of the juvenile court, the Supreme Court acknowledged that juveniles often did not receive care and treatment in actual practice. If the Supreme Court's reform changed the actual practice of the juvenile court, then we would expect to find an increase in care and treatment since that time. If we do not find such an increase, then it would be clear that the Supreme Court's new conception of the juvenile court was not implemented in actual practice and that the juvenile court itself continues to violate the equal protection clause of the Constitution.

Actual Changes in Disposition Hearings

The "war on crime" burst onto the political scene shortly after the Supreme Court began making its decisions on the juvenile court in 1966.

This political movement resulted in a great deal of "get tough" legislation about crime, some aimed at juveniles and the juvenile court. The focus shifted to serious juvenile offenders—those who murdered and raped and robbed. Juvenile court was portrayed as a "kiddie court" that tapped such serious offenders on the wrist and told them to be good little boys.[17] These juveniles would piously agree to be good and were released before the police officer had finished filling out the forms. As soon as they were out the door, the juveniles would murder and rape and rob again.

By 1975, when the *Breed* v. *Jones* decision completed the Supreme Court's set of rulings, state legislatures across the country had already begun passing laws that "toughened up" this kiddie court. Because there were fifty different state legislatures, a great deal of diversity characterized the laws that were passed. Thus, the main effect of these new laws was to dynamite the nationwide uniformity in handling juvenile offenders that had resulted from the unanimous adoption of the original juvenile court.[18]

There was one general trend, however. Most of the legislatures directed their attention to the disposition phase, demanding the serious juvenile offenders be punished rather than treated.[19] Laws describing the purpose of the juvenile court were changed to include the punishment of offenders, not just treatment and best interests of the juvenile. Various mandatory sentences were passed for particular kinds of crimes. The number of ways to transfer juveniles to criminal court was increased, where juveniles presumably would be treated more harshly. Some of those waivers were made mandatory. Jurisdiction over some offenses was transferred out of the juvenile court all together and placed in criminal court, and some states provided the death penalty for juvenile offenders.

The "solicitous care" that would be felt by a kindly parent for a wayward child was replaced by anger and hostility and rage. The "regenerative treatment" juveniles were to receive from the juvenile court was instead punishment and retribution. This "best" aspect of the original juvenile court withered away in an onslaught of fear and frustration.

Legislators seemed to have their own version of the "best of both worlds": serious offenders were to receive punishment for their offenses in the disposition phase, while minor offenders would continue to receive the "solicitous care and regenerative treatment" that would be provided by a kindly parent. The "best of both worlds," in the legislators' view, seemed to be treatment for minor offenders and punishment for serious ones.

Over time, this "tough" version of the "best of both worlds" became even tougher. The juvenile court became increasingly oriented toward punishment, and a separate trend developed to divert minor and status offenders to the voluntary treatment agencies. Especially in larger cities, juvenile courts got out of the treatment business all together and began to conceive of their jobs solely in terms of punishing offenders. In those places, the juvenile court no longer could be described as the "best of both worlds" because all resemblance to the original juvenile court had faded away. What remained was a junior criminal court whose major difference with the adult criminal court is that they provide fewer due process rights in the adjudication hearing and (generally speaking) less punishment in the disposition hearing.

The Lessons of History

In practice, juveniles acquired few legal protections in adjudication hearings because there are few such hearings to begin with and most of those are "show trials" in which adjudication is a foregone conclusion. Juveniles, parents, and defense attorneys are unable to resist this procedure because juries and appeals are not available. In practice, juveniles also lost a fair portion of the treatment that they were receiving at the time of the Supreme Court decisions. The Court had noted that juveniles did not actually receive much treatment then, but they receive even less treatment now.

The Supreme Court's reform simply did not "sell" with the general public. What "sold" instead was the "get tough" movement. The Supreme Court's reform did not fit well with the "lessons of history" presented at the end of Chapter 5, but consider how well the "get tough" movement fits with those same lessons.

Lesson 1: The Cycle of Juvenile Justice
>   High juvenile crime rates are accompanied by a belief that
>   these rates can be lowered by appropriate juvenile justice
>   policies. This results in a continuous cycle of reform. The
>   cycle itself consists in establishing lenient treatments in a
>   major reform, gradually "toughening up" those treatments

over a long time so that officials end up choosing between harsh punishments and doing nothing at all, and then reestablishing lenient treatments in another major reform.

The "get tough" movement fits nicely into this cycle. At the present time, juvenile justice officials still have lenient options and are not faced with the forced choice between harsh punishments and doing nothing at all. Thus, policies that toughen up those responses in order to solve the problem of delinquency are the ones that should "sell." This is precisely what the "get tough" movement offers.

If this cycle continues, we should expect that juvenile justice officials eventually will no longer have any lenient options left and will confront the same forced choice that faced officials in New York in 1825 and Chicago in 1899: either harshly punish or do nothing. At that point, the system will be prepared for another major structural reform in which lenient treatments are once again introduced into juvenile justice.

Lesson 2: Ideas of Juvenile Delinquency

Ideas of delinquency that "sell" (i.e., that succeed in the competition with other possible ideas) propose that delinquents are a subgroup within some larger problem group (e.g., paupers, dependent and neglected children) with which the public is already familiar.

Lesson 3: Ideas of Juvenile Justice

Responses to delinquency that "sell" (i.e., that succeed in the competition with other possible responses) are slightly modified versions of responses to the larger problem group of which delinquents are thought to be a subgroup.

The "war on crime" had provided an idea of the criminal as a vicious and depraved maniac who should be locked up for the protection of society. This idea became well known and widely accepted among the general public. The "get tough" movement proposed that juvenile delinquents were a subgroup within this larger problem group. As *Time* Magazine put it, delinquents were "remorseless, mutant juvenile(s)" who are "robbing and raping, maiming and murdering as casually as they go to a movie or join a pickup baseball game."[20] The response to juvenile delinquents therefore was a slight modification of the response to that broader group: lock them up and throw away the key. All this is consistent with Lessons 2 and 3.

Lesson 4: Economic Interests of the Rich and Powerful
    Responses to delinquency that "sell" attempt to change the
    behavior of poor and powerless people but not the behavior of
    rich and powerful people. In particular, these responses do not
    harm the economic interests of the rich and powerful.

The "get tough" movement was consistent with this lesson, since it
focused on changing the behavior of delinquents and proposed nothing
that affected the rich and powerful.

Lesson 5: Moral and Intellectual Superiority of Reformers
    Responses to delinquency that "sell" imply that delinquents
    and their parents are morally and intellectually inferior, and
    that the reformers are morally and intellectually superior.

The "get tough" movement portrayed juvenile delinquents as depraved and vicious subhumans, remorseless mutants who casually murdered and raped and robbed. Such depictions surely implied that they
were morally and intellectually inferior. Once delinquents are portrayed
in that way, then it is natural to infer that the reformers themselves are
superior, at least to the delinquents.
    The sense of superiority among the reformers went beyond that simple
inference, however. Unlike the Founders of the United States government, the proponents of this movement did not express any concern that
innocent juveniles might be adjudicated and severely punished. Instead,
they expressed a clear and unquestioned sense that they had intellectual
ability to identify the truly vicious and depraved delinquents and the
moral virtue to punish those offenders with righteous indignation. It was
precisely this kind of arrogance among officials that the Founders feared
and tried to inhibit through mechanisms such as due process protections.

Lesson 6: The "Unfair Comparison"
    Reformers "sell" their own reforms by an "unfair compari-
    son" in which a harsh assessment of the actual practices of
    past policies is compared with an optimistic assessment of the
    new reform, based on their own good intentions. Because they
    assume that their good intentions directly translate into actual
    practice, reformers more or less promise to "solve" the
    problem of delinquency.

Like other reformers, the "get tough" reformers engaged in the "unfair comparison" by exaggerating the problems of the old juvenile justice system, based on a harsh assessment of its actual practices. They also exaggerated the wonderful results of their proposed system, based entirely on their good intentions. These reformers suggest that their good intentions (severely punish serious offenders) could be directly translated into actual practices. In reality, however, these laws resulted in a whole host of complex problems that compromised their effectiveness.

In particular, "criminal justice thermodynamics"[21] took over: the increase in the severity of the penalty resulted in a decline in its application. For example, New York State passed an extremely harsh "Juvenile Offender Law" that required mandatory waivers to adult court and lengthy sentences for juveniles as young as 13 who commit a variety of serious offenses. This law was so severe that processing these cases came to a virtual halt in most of the state.[22]

Lesson 7: The Power of the State

> Reforms that "sell" increase the power of the state, based on the optimistic assessment of how effective the reform will be in "solving" the problem of delinquency, and on the (presumed) moral and intellectual superiority of the reformers.

The "get tough" movement certainly increased the power of the State in comparison to the Supreme Court's decisions, which had attempted to restrict that same power. But it also increased that power in comparison to the original juvenile court. The "get tough" movement relieved the state of the obligation to determine the best interests of juveniles, to care for them and treat their problems. The state gained the freedom to punish juveniles without concern for their welfare. In that sense, the power of the state expanded.

Conclusion

The Supreme Court's idea was to give juveniles the best of both worlds—treatment with due process. Instead, the "get tough" movement gave juveniles the worst of both worlds—punishment without due process.

This has moved us a long way back to the situation existing before the founding of the first juvenile court. At that time, there were only two ways to respond to juveniles who got into trouble: voluntary treatment in private social agencies and coerced punishment in the criminal courts. The founders of the juvenile court added a new option they believed would be uniquely appropriate for these juveniles: *coerced treatment* in the new juvenile court.

At present, this option is in danger of disappearing. If the trend continues, then juvenile court judges soon will be faced with the forced choice between harshly punishing and doing nothing at all.

Notes

1. Frederic L. Faust and Paul J. Brantingham, *Juvenile Justice Philosophy*, West, St. Paul, 1979, p. 383.

2. In that sense, Fortas' description was actually one side of an "unfair comparison"—i.e., it was an excessively pessimistic view of actual practices in the past. Fortas then went on to give the other side of that comparison—an excessively optimistic view of what would happen in the future, based on his own good intentions.

3. H. Ted Rubin, *Juvenile Justice*, 2nd ed., Random House, New York, 1985; Rubin, "The Juvenile Court Landscape," in Albert R. Roberts, *Juvenile Justice*, Dorsey, Chicago, 1989, p. 129.

4. James T. Carey and Patrick D. McAnany, *Introduction to Juvenile Delinquency*, Prentice-Hall, Englewood Cliffs, 1984, pp. 267–68.

5. Thomas Grisso, *Juveniles' Waiver of Rights*, Plenum, New York, 1981.

6. Rubin, op. cit., 1985.

7. Grisso, op. cit., Chapter 8.

8. Rubin, op. cit., 1985, 1989; M. A. Bortner, *Inside Juvenile Court*, New York University Press, New York, 1982.

9. Bortner, op. cit., p. 45.

10. Carey and McAnany, op. cit., p. 268.

11. Howard N. Snyder et al., *Juvenile Court Statistics, 1984*. National Center for Juvenile Justice, Pittsburgh, 1987, p. 16.

12. Charles Silberman, *Criminal Violence, Criminal Justice*, Random House, New York, 1978, pp. 279–80.

13. Carey and McAnany, op. cit., p. 269; see also W. Vaughan Stapleton and Lee E. Teitlebaum, *In Defense of Youth*, Russell Sage, New York, 1972, Chapter 5.

14. Cary and McAnany, op. cit., pp. 270–72.

15. Patrick Murphy, *Our Kindly Parent, The State*, Viking, New York, 1974.

16. The "equal protection" theory is reviewed above in the discussion of the Kent (pp. 112–13) and Gault (p. 117) cases.

17. E.g., see "The Youth Crime Plague," *Time* Magazine, July 11, 1977, pp. 18–28.

18. Thomas J. Bernard and Daniel Katkin, "Introduction," *Law & Policy* 8(4):391–95 (October, 1986).

19. See Rubin, op. cit., 1985, Chapter 2.

20. *Time* Magazine, op. cit., p. 18.

21. Samuel Walker, *Sense and Nonsense About Crime,* Brooks/Cole, Pacific Grove, 1989, pp. 46–48. See also pp. 36–37 above for a discussion of this concept.

22. Simon I. Singer and Charles Patrick Ewing, "Juvenile Justice Reform in New York State: The Juvenile Offender Law," *Law & Policy* 8(4):463–78 (October, 1986).

9

The Lessons of History

Predictions vs. Prescriptions

This book looks at the history of juvenile delinquency and juvenile justice to see if some lessons from the past might be applied to the present and the future. In this chapter, I state what I think those lessons are. There are two types of lessons we can learn from the past: predictions and prescriptions.

Predictions assume people never learn anything from history and that they simply repeat the mistakes of the past over and over again. These lessons answer the question: If people are unwilling to learn from the past and tend to repeat it, what can we expect to happen in the future?

Predictions are relatively straightforward since they involve analysis of past historical patterns and the projection of those patterns into the future. If we figure out what the cyclical patterns were in the past, then we simply predict that people will continue to repeat those patterns in the future.

Prescriptions, in contrast, are based on an attempt to learn from history and chart a better course. They attempt to answer the question: If we really could learn from the past, what would we do differently in the present and future?

Prescriptions are more complex because they involve value judgments about the past: what was good or bad, right or wrong, just or unjust, better or worse, important or unimportant. Ultimately, these lessons involve judgments about what is possible or impossible in the present and future. So prescriptions are more likely to provoke disagreement than predictions.

Predictions: The Cycle Continues

A cyclical pattern has been identified in past juvenile justice policies, generated by several aspects of juvenile justice that have stayed the same over the last two hundred years. My prediction is that this cycle of juvenile justice will continue in the future.

Juveniles will continue to be a high crime rate group, and they also will continue to receive less punishment than adults who commit the same offenses. Adults will continue to be convinced that there is a "juvenile crime wave" that started in the last thirty or forty years, and they will continue to believe that lenient punishments are the cause of that crime wave.

Thus, there will be continuing pressure to increase the punishments of juvenile offenders and limit and eliminate the possibility of responding with leniency. We have already come a fair distance down this road, and justice officials eventually will reach the point when they have only harsh punishments available for responding to delinquents. They then will be forced to choose between applying those harsh punishments and doing nothing at all. We will live with that situation for some time, but juvenile crime rates will remain high.

At some point, a new group of reformers will come along and blame those high crime rates on the "forced choice" between harsh punishments and doing nothing. These reformers will propose a new "idea" of juvenile delinquency: juveniles will be described as a subgroup of some larger problem group familiar to the public. This will allow the public to assimilate the new "idea of juvenile delinquency" easily, to believe that it is innovative, creative, and different while still not being required to think anything that they did not already think. There will already be an established method for dealing with this larger problem group, and the public will also be familiar with it. The reformers then will propose a method for dealing with delinquents that is a modified version of that method. This will enable the public both to treat this reform as new and innovative and creative, and at the same time not require them to think anything that is really new and different.

Whatever the content of this new idea, its function will be to reintroduce leniency in the responses to juvenile offenders. That is, its function will be to fill the gap between harshly punishing and doing nothing at all.

The reformers will promise that the new methods more or less will solve the problem of delinquency. They will sell the reform by harshly criticizing the actual practices of the existing (''get tough'') system, and optimistically asserting that their own good intentions can be translated into actual practices with few short-range and no long-range problems.

One can expect that this new reform will require an expansion of state power. In particular, the new methods will probably trample the few due process rights that juveniles acquired in practice as a result of the decisions by the United States Supreme Court. However, the reformers will argue that it is appropriate to ignore these rights because the juveniles are being helped and not punished.

Eventually, a test case will go up on appeal, and the courts will have to confront whether this trampling of rights is constitutional. At this point, we can expect a new Crouse-type decision. Using the new philosophy and the new optimism generated by it, a court will approve this further expansion of state power. The language and logic of Crouse and Fisher will live again, and the language and logic of O'Connell and Gault once again will be confined to the dustbin of history.

After the reform is implemented, a ''honeymoon'' period will last for some time, during which people will optimistically believe the new system works wonderfully. Inevitably, however, this system will confront the same problems the old system confronted. Juveniles will remain a high crime rate group, and adults will remain convinced that this problem began only recently. After enough time has passed, adults will begin to blame the ''juvenile crime wave'' on the new system instead of the old one. In particular, they will blame the leniency with which delinquents are being treated. Of course, the whole point of the new system was to reintroduce leniency to avoid the ''forced choice'' between harshly punishing and doing nothing at all, but that will have been forgotten. The system will start to ''toughen up'' its responses, and the gradual and lengthy trip back to the ''forced choice'' between harsh punishments and doing nothing will begin again.

Prescriptions: The Best and the Worst of Each Policy

People normally do not learn anything from history, and so I believe that juvenile justice policy is likely to continue cycling through the sequence of stages described above. But I also have thoughts about what we might do to break that cycle and establish a stable policy. This involves examining each of the various policies within the cycle and determining their best and worst aspects. The stable policy could then be constructed by combining the best aspects of each policy.

Because value judgments are involved, different people will have different ideas about what is best and what is worst. The following are my own ideas on that subject. They are organized as a discussion of each "idea of juvenile delinquency" and its associated "idea of juvenile justice." After this discussion, I combine these ideas into a proposed "best" policy for juvenile justice.

No Idea of Juvenile Delinquency

Before the establishment of the first juvenile institution, there was no idea of juvenile delinquency at all. Once children were 6 or 7, they were viewed as people like everyone else, and when they violated the law, they were viewed as criminals like everyone else. The response to juvenile delinquents therefore was a modified version of the response to adult criminals: punishments mitigated because of age.

There were two "best" aspects of this policy that should be retained in any future juvenile justice policy. One was the assumption that, under normal circumstances and with exceptions, juveniles were entitled to receive less punishment than adults for the same offenses. This was not questioned as a policy that benefited both the juvenile and the larger society, since most juveniles took advantage of the reduced punishments to stop committing crimes. Second, juveniles had as many rights in criminal court as adults. Neither group had many rights in practice, but juveniles were not given fewer rights than adults.

The worst aspect of this policy was that punishment was the only available response. The choice was limited to punishing the juvenile, even if it was mitigated, or doing nothing at all. With that choice, officials often refused to punish at all because they believed that punishment might increase juvenile crime.

Juvenile Delinquents as Potential Paupers

The term "juvenile delinquent" originated with the idea that these youths were potential paupers, and the term itself conveys that meaning. At the time the term originated, pauperism was the subject of a lot of public attention, so that this new "idea of juvenile delinquency" was easily assimilated by the general public. The associated policy response (the "idea of juvenile justice") therefore was a modified version of the policy response to paupers: institutionalize them to teach them good work habits and then apprentice them out until they became adults.

The best aspect of this policy is suggested by the term "potential." It implies that children are not fixed and "hardened" but in a process of becoming something else. In this case, it was suggested that they were becoming paupers, but this was a more specific version of the idea that children were in the process of becoming adults. Thus, the term "potential" reflected the second conception of childhood as the basis for the idea of juvenile delinquency.

The policy response associated with this notion was that this developmental process could be modified, that such children could be shaped and molded and "re-formed" into law-abiding citizens by juvenile justice policy. It is this optimistic attitude that we are losing today with the current conception of juvenile delinquents as "hardened criminals."

The worst aspect of this policy is the idea that juvenile delinquents can be reformed by placing them in institutions, and that the problem of juvenile delinquency itself could be solved without any other action. From their very beginnings, institutions have failed to accomplish this task, and this failure has been exceedingly costly in human and financial terms.

Recently, institutions have begun to lose their central position in the juvenile justice system. In 1970, Massachusetts substituted an extensive network of community services as its central response to delinquency.[1] Most of those services are purchased from private agencies rather than provided by state employees.[2] All large juvenile institutions have been closed and a number of small (the largest facility holds eighteen juveniles) secure facilities were opened for juveniles too dangerous to be left on the streets. These secure facilities provide extensive treatment services. For example, the eighteen-bed facility has a full-time counselor supervisor and three full-time counselors, each with a caseload of six. Many institutions with five hundred juveniles would consider themselves lucky to have such a large counseling staff.

Since this policy took effect, Massachusetts' delinquency rates have declined substantially in comparison to states that rely heavily on institutions, such as Florida.[3] Utah and more recently Nebraska have now followed Massachusetts' lead.[4]

Recent research suggests that community corrections is at least as

effective as institutional corrections as the response to most delinquency,[5] and that small treatment-oriented secure facilities are more
effective than large institutions in reforming the few dangerous juvenile
offenders who require confinement.[6] Thus, the reliance on large institutions that began with reformers in New York in 1825 seems to have been a
great mistake.

An even greater mistake is the idea that juvenile justice policy alone
can solve the problem of delinquency. While Massachusetts' juvenile
justice system may be more effective than Florida's, it cannot "solve"
the problem of delinquency either. The solution to this problem requires
changes in the larger social and economic conditions in society. Those
conditions, such as in New York in 1825 and Chicago in 1899, gave rise
to the modern problem of juvenile delinquency in the first place. This
problem did not arise because of inadequate or ineffective juvenile justice
policies, and it will not disappear if adequate and effective policies are
instituted.

Juvenile Delinquents as Dependent and Neglected Children

The next idea of juvenile delinquency was a modified version of the idea
of dependent and neglected children: delinquents lacked proper parental
care and support. A great deal of public attention had been devoted to
dependent and neglected children at that time as a result of the expanding
child welfare movement. Therefore, this new "idea of juvenile delinquency" was easily assimilated by the general public. The associated
policy response (the "idea of juvenile justice") was a modified version of
the response to dependent and neglected children. If the natural parents
did not provide proper care and supervision for these children, then the
state (as *parens patriae*) would do so.

There are five "best" aspects of this reform that I would keep in a
"best" juvenile justice system. The first is the idea of linking delinquency to parental care and supervision. The founders of the juvenile
court believed that dependency is the natural state of all children and that
delinquency is only one of many manifestations of the lack of proper care
and supervision. Recent research suggests there is considerable truth to
that view.[7]

Establishment of the juvenile court was a second "best" aspect of this
policy. Earlier responses were limited to voluntary treatments in private
agencies or coercive punishments in criminal court. The juvenile court

added a third option: coercive treatments. This option is particularly appropriate for children because they are still in the process of development (the second idea of childhood) and are not "hardened" criminals.

The third "best" aspect was the idea that the juvenile court should act in the best interests of the child. Today, the "get tough" movement often demands that we harm the child to protect the interests of the larger society. The founders of the juvenile court would have described this as extraordinarily short-sighted. They saw no conflict between society's interests and those of the child. They believed society's long-term interests are always served by protecting the child. This idea deserves to be kept in any future juvenile system.

A fourth "best" aspect was the legal definition that juveniles could not form criminal intent (*mens rea*). Since the dawn of time, age always has been a factor believed to influence the ability to form criminal intent. The juvenile court extended this concept by applying it to all juveniles rather than only to those under age 7. This is the legal mechanism that removes juveniles from criminal court jurisdiction and allows them to be processed under a system oriented to their best interests rather than to punishment. I believe this should be retained in future juvenile justice systems whether or not it has any merit as a literal description of adolescent psychology. That is, I would treat this as a convenient "legal fiction" that allows the juvenile justice system to exist.[8]

A fifth "best" aspect is the new language system that reflects the structure and function of a social welfare agency rather than a criminal court. To a certain extent, this language masks the true criminal functions of the juvenile court, but it also operates as a symbol that shapes the thinking and behavior of the people who work in the court. In a world full of symbols that push people toward punishment of juveniles, the language of treatment in juvenile justice seems worth retaining, even if reality does not always live up to the intentions.

The worst aspect of this policy was eliminating the juvenile's due process rights. In practice, juveniles had few due process rights before the establishment of the first juvenile court, but after its establishment, they had no rights even in theory. As with the language of social welfare, the theoretical existence of these rights was useful even if reality did not always correspond. Thus, I regard the elimination of these rights as a mistake.

Juvenile Delinquents as Criminal Defendants

In their series of decisions beginning with Kent and Gault, the United States Supreme Court proposed an "idea of juvenile delinquency" that was a modified version of the way they were looking at criminal defendants at the time. Their "idea of juvenile justice" therefore was a modified version of their policy response to adult criminals: provide juveniles with some (but not all) of the due process rights given to adults.

The best aspect of this policy is that it reintroduces due process rights for juvenile delinquents. It links coercive treatment with restrictions on the state's power, and suggests that juveniles need protection from the state even if the state acts in the juvenile's best interest.

There are two aspects that I regard as "worsts" in the sense that they should not be included in any future hypothetical juvenile justice policy. Both are related to the fact that the Supreme Court's reform was logical and rational and "made sense" for the juvenile justice system (i.e., it was based on a coherent philosophy) but it did not consider how that system actually performed in its day-to-day activities.

The first "worst" aspect is that, for various reasons, the due process rights of juveniles were not effective in practice. The Supreme Court did not provide either jury trial, the right to treatment, or a practical means of appeal to juveniles. As a result, almost all juveniles are found to have committed the offense for which they were referred to the court. This means that, in practice, the power of the state is not limited in its relation to juveniles and juveniles have no effective due process rights. This "worst" aspect therefore nullifies in practice the "best" aspect of the Supreme Court's reform.

The second "worst" aspect is that the Supreme Court failed to ensure that juveniles actually receive treatment in the disposition phase. The Supreme Court correctly observed that juveniles had been punished and not treated in the past, but then they based their constitutional argument on the assumption that juveniles would be treated and not punished in the future. This assumption was unrealistic in the light of how things are really done.

Both of these "worst" aspects would have been eliminated by a practical and effective right to treatment. In essence, such a right means that if juveniles demonstrate that they are not being treated by the juvenile justice system, then they must be released from the jurisdiction of the juvenile court.

This right would have assured that juveniles were actually helped if they were adjudicated, not merely punished for their offenses. That would have solved the equal protection problem that continues to challenge the constitutionality of the juvenile court: juveniles receive less protection from the law but obtain no special benefits that compensates them for this loss. It also would have been a single but effective due process right, where the other due process rights are ineffective in practice. The idea of a practical and effective right to treatment will be further discussed below.

Juvenile Delinquents as Hardened Criminals

The "get tough" movement has proposed the idea that juvenile delinquents are hardened criminals. Such criminals have been the subject of a great deal of public attention in the last twenty years as part of the continuing "war on crime," and so this new "idea of juvenile delinquency" has been easily assimilated by the general public. The associated "idea of juvenile justice" therefore is a modified version of the policy response to dangerous criminals: lock them up for extended periods of time to prevent them from preying on innocent victims.

Some similarity is evident between this recent view and the one that prevailed before the establishment of the first juvenile institution, when there was no "idea of juvenile delinquency." In fact, the current view is much more severe. Two hundred years ago, it was commonly acknowledged that most juvenile crime was minor and nonserious, and that most juvenile criminals were best dealt with by punishing them less than adults who commit the same offenses. The assumption was that juveniles would take advantage of this leniency to "get out while the getting was good." Thus, mitigation was not questioned as the basic response to juvenile offending.

Today, the view of juveniles as "hardened criminals" suggests that mitigation is inappropriate and foolish. "Get tough" advocates argue that juveniles use leniency as an opportunity to commit more frequent and serious offenses without fear of the consequences, rather than as an opportunity to "get out while the getting is good." Thus, this current "idea of juvenile delinquency" is considerably "tougher" than the one two hundred years ago.

The best aspect of this idea is that at least some juveniles can form criminal intent and therefore deserve full punishment for the offenses

TABLE 7. The Best and the Worst Aspects of Each Idea

Idea of juvenile delinquency	Idea of juvenile justice	
	Best aspects	*Worst aspects*
No idea of juvenile delinquency	Mitigated punishments Full due process	Punishment was the only option
Delinquents as potential paupers	Developmental conception of childhood Optimism about reforming juveniles	Juvenile justice can solve problem of delinquency Institutions can reform delinquents
Delinquents as dependent and neglected children	Delinquency tied to parental care Juvenile court as coercive treatment Best interest, not punishment No *mens rea* Language of social welfare	No due process rights
Delinquents as criminal defendants	Some formal due process rights	No due process in practice No assurance of treatment
Delinquents as hardened criminals	Serious offenders deserve serious punishment	Inappropriate for vast majority of offenders Serious offenders respond better to treatment than to punishment

they commit. The original juvenile institutions and the original juvenile court were designed to deal with minor offenders, but as the cycle of juvenile justice progressed, both increasingly handled serious offenders and ignored the minor offenders they were designed to handle. The "get tough" movement may be correct in arguing that very serious criminals do not belong in the juvenile justice system.

The "worst" aspect of this reform is that punishing serious juvenile offenders may actually increase crime. Research suggests that recidivism among the most violent delinquents can be reduced up to 70% in small, secure, treatment-oriented juvenile facilities.[8] This same type of juvenile does poorly when punished in large custody-oriented juvenile institutions.[9] The adult system has even less to offer these offenders and they cause many problems in it, both as victims and offenders.[10]

A second "worst" aspect is that get-tough reformers would discard many advances that juvenile justice has made over the last two hundred years. They would abandon the developmental conception of childhood and return to the view that juveniles are simply smaller adults. They would eliminate coerced treatment as a particularly appropriate method of dealing with children, and restrict the court's options to either punishing delinquents or doing nothing at all. This is an untenable position and, as the cycle of juvenile justice continues, it inevitably would lead to the reestablishment of leniency in a new major reform.

Ultimately, the "get tough" reformers want to design the juvenile justice system to deal only with hardened criminals who take advantage of leniency in order to commit more henious crimes. But these are a tiny minority of the juveniles handled by the juvenile justice system. The overwhelming majority are minor and occasional offenders who (sooner or later) use leniency as an opportunity to refrain from further offending. The juvenile justice system should be designed to deal with the overwhelming majority of juvenile offenders, not with a tiny minority.

Breaking the Cycle of Juvenile Justice

Historical and Philosophical Context

We study history to be able to see ourselves in a historical and philosophical context. In this instance, our *historical context* is the cycle of juvenile justice: the introduction of leniency in a major reform, a gradual toughening up until officials must choose between imposing harsh punishments and doing nothing, and then the reintroduction of leniency in another major reform. At the present time, we are somewhere in the "toughening up" process. Only by studying history can we realize our place in this cycle. Otherwise, we see only the present policy and the need to move to the next policy in the cycle.

The historical context is driven by our *philosophical context*—that is, shared rational and coherent ideas that "hang together" and make sense. This philosophical context includes the ideas that juvenile crime is exceptionally high, that the problem is recent and did not exist in the "good old days," and that the cause of this problem lies in current justice policies. It also includes the "unfair comparison," in which a harsh assessment of the actual practices of past policies is compared to an optimistic assessment of future policies, based on the good intentions of the reformers.

Only by studying history can we put these ideas in their historical context: they have remained the same for at least two hundred years. They have been popular whether existing juvenile justice policies are harsh or lenient, whether the proposed policies are harsh or lenient, and whether juvenile delinquency itself is somewhat higher or somewhat lower. Thus, these ideas are like a stopped clock: they say the same thing all the time, so they are right some of the time and wrong most of the time.

The Cycle of Juvenile Justice

Because of these ideas, people continually expect juvenile justice policies to reduce juvenile crime. They therefore reform or discard any policy that fails to accomplish that task.

But no policy has been able to accomplish this. Juveniles have always been a high-crime-rate group, going back to when Cain killed Abel. If the past establishes a baseline for what to expect in the future, then we can expect that juveniles are always going to be a high-crime-rate group. Because every policy fails to reduce juvenile crime, every policy is eventually reformed and the cycle of juvenile justice continues.

The "Best" Juvenile Justice Policy

The cycle of juvenile justice cannot be broken by any particular juvenile justice policy, since all policies eventually are broken by the cycle. The only way to break the cycle is to change the philosophic context: the belief that an as-yet undiscovered juvenile justice policy will transform juveniles into a low-crime-rate group.

If the public could give up its belief in such a policy, we could make reasonable choices among the various real policies for dealing with juveniles. Such a choice must be based on a "fair comparison" rather than an unfair one. That is, we would choose among the various policies at various stages of the cycle, based on a comparison of their actual practices, not their good intentions. My own recommendations about such choices are presented below. I would make three preliminary arguments here.

First, the cycle of juvenile justice cannot be broken unless juvenile justice policies include leniency for at least some juvenile offenders. A policy that does not include any leniency inevitably results in a "forced choice" between harshly punishing and doing nothing. Given that choice, "criminal justice thermodynamics" takes over and many juveniles are let off scot-free, which then results in pressure to reform the system by introducing leniency. Thus, the cycle of juvenile justice continues.

Second, once we choose the extent to which leniency is available, then we must expect that a certain portion of the juveniles receiving leniency will go on to commit serious offenses. We will then be tempted to "toughen up" the leniency to further reduce juvenile crime. To do so would continue the cycle of juvenile justice. The belief that tougher penalties reduce juvenile crime is based on an "unfair comparison" because in actual practice a certain portion of juveniles receiving tougher penalties also go on to commit serious crime. If we go that route, we ultimately will end up back where officials must choose between harsh punishments and doing nothing, and then a new reform will reintroduce leniency.

Third, the cycle of juvenile justice cannot be broken unless our ideas about juvenile delinquency and juvenile justice are changed. Those ideas drive the cycle, and they will break any particular policy that is put into place by reformers. Thus, my recommendations focus more on changing our ideas about juvenile delinquency and juvenile justice than on changing the juvenile justice system.

An "Idea of Juvenile Delinquency": Naive Risk-taking

Earlier Ideas of Delinquency Are Inappropriate

Juvenile justice policies are based on "ideas" of the juvenile delinquent that involve relatively simple analogies to other well-known problem groups. The four examined in this book are juvenile delinquents as potential paupers, dependent and neglected children, presumably innocent defendants with rights, and hardened criminals. Each of these ideas is appropriate for some juvenile offenders but inappropriate for most others.

Some juvenile offenders are "potential paupers" but most, with no intervention at all or minimal intervention by juvenile justice officials, grow up and settle down and hold jobs and pay taxes.[11] Many of these same people later demand tough penalties for juvenile offenders. They forget that they received leniency themselves, that they might have been sent to an institution if tough policies had been in effect when they were young. Thus, while some juvenile delinquents are "potential paupers," most are not.

Some juvenile offenders are dependent and neglected children, but most have imperfect and fallible parents who do their best under difficult circumstances. These parents love their children and try to get them to obey the law, even if they sometimes do so in ways that make the problem worse. It can be helpful to train these parents in more effective parenting techniques,[12] but it is wrong to describe most delinquents as dependent or neglected children.

Some juvenile offenders are presumably innocent defendants with due process rights, but most are not defendants at all because they never have an adjudication hearing. The police only arrest between 20% and 50% of the juveniles they accuse of committing crimes, and they only refer about half of those they arrest to the juvenile court.[13] The juvenile court only holds adjudication hearings for about 5% of the juveniles referred to it. So well under 1% of juveniles accused of crimes by the police ever receive an adjudication hearing. In practice, the vast majority of juvenile delinquents are never defendants at all, much less defendants with rights.

Finally, some juveniles are hardened criminals, but most are adolescents acting the way adolescents always have: wild and crazy. After years of being children under the control of adults, they suddenly find they have the freedom to do what they want and adults can't stop them. They celebrate their freedom with exuberance and joy, but they have not yet learned that their actions can have hurtful consequences. They believe they can take all kinds of risks and nothing will ever happen to them. Like Superman, they think bullets bounce off their chest. Adults warn them about the consequences of their actions, even yell and scream and threaten. But the adolescents laugh it off and ignore it. They are having a good time.

Sooner or later, the consequences actually happen, either to them or to their friends. Someone flunks out of school and is kicked out of the house and takes a dead-end job or can't get a job at all. Someone overdoses on drugs and suffers permanent brain damage. Someone is seriously injured or killed while driving drunk. Reality rears its ugly head, and the adolescents are overwhelmed. Where before they felt confident and joyful, now they feel vulnerable and frightened: that could happen to me, too.

This process is called "growing up." All adults have been through it, and no matter how hard they try to save adolescents from the pain and danger of the experience, most need to experience it themselves. Experience, after all, is the best teacher.

A New Idea of Juvenile Delinquency

Research shows that juvenile delinquency is a complex phenomenon, not reducible to any simple image.[14] But the public demands such an image, and juvenile justice policies will be based on one whether I like it or not. Therefore, I offer my own "idea of juvenile delinquency," one that I think is appropriate for the vast majority of juvenile offenders: the juvenile delinquent as a *naive risk-taker.*

Most adolescents, including most juvenile delinquents, are "naive" in the sense that they do not understand that actions have consequences.[15] Most delinquency arises from this tendency toward risk-taking behavior.[16] Adolescents "age out" of juvenile delinquency for the same reason they "age out" of other forms of risk-taking: either they or their friends suffer the consequences of their actions.[17] Then they are no longer "naive." All of us learn this as we grow up. Some of us learn it without suffering permanent damage, but others experience losses that affect the rest of their lives.

Naive Risk-taking and Mens Rea

The idea of juvenile delinquents as naive risk-takers is consistent with the position taken by the founders of the juvenile court that juveniles lack *mens rea* or the guilty mind. *Mens rea* is a confusing concept that has been defined in many different ways. Most of those definitions, however, focus on an awareness of the consequences of criminal actions.[18] An offender who lacks this awareness cannot be considered "blameworthy" and therefore cannot be said to have *mens rea.*

If delinquents are defined as people who do not fully understand the consequences of their actions, then they cannot fully understand the consequences that their criminal actions have for their victims. For example, in cases where a juvenile has killed another person, the issue in a waiver hearing usually is whether the juvenile has a sense of what it is to take a life. At least some younger juveniles have little sense of death and a TV image of cops and robbers shooting everyone in sight. Juveniles who really do not understand death cannot form criminal intention in the traditional meaning of the term.

I am suggesting that there are two different meanings to the statement that juveniles may not fully understand the consequences of their actions. First, they may not fully understand the consequences of their criminal actions for victims in terms of physical and psychological injuries and traumas. Second, they may not fully understand the consequences of their criminal actions for themselves, in terms of the possibility that they may be caught and punished, with consequences that could affect the remainder of their lives.

Juvenile Offenders Who Are Rational Calculators

Some youthful offenders are not naive risk-takers and are fully aware of the consequences of their actions. They do not care about the consequences of their criminal actions to victims (e.g., physical or psychological trauma) and they rationally calculate whether they want to take a chance on the consequences of their actions to themselves (e.g., being sent to prison). As such, they are capable of forming criminal intention and should be subject to the full punishments associated with their crimes. These offenders can be described as "rational calculators" because they rationally calculate the benefits of crime and weigh it against the possible punishments if they are caught.[19]

Such youths, in my opinion, should NOT be described as "juvenile delinquents" and do NOT belong in a juvenile justice system based on the idea of the delinquent as a naive risk-taker. These offenders are young criminals and should be processed in criminal court. The criminal court, after all, assumes that criminals are rational calculators and sets its penalties accordingly.

I believe that there are very few such juvenile offenders, whereas the "get tough" reformers believe there are very many. While that is a point of disagreement, I agree with these reformers in arguing that such offenders should be transferred to criminal court. I disagree with these reformers when they argue that the juvenile justice system should be reformed so that it is designed to handle such offenders. My principal argument here is that the juvenile justice system should be based on an idea of the juvenile delinquent as a naive risk-taker. Juveniles who are not naive risk-takers, who are better described as rationally calculating young criminals, should be transferred to the criminal justice system.

An "Idea of Juvenile Justice": Communication

If juvenile delinquency is defined in terms of naive risk-taking, the function of the juvenile justice system should be to communicate that actions have consequences. Such communication should involve the minimum consequences possible. That is, the extent of the consequences should be determined by the need to communicate with the juvenile, not by the nature of the offense.

The initial attempt to communicate should be through *threats*. If those fail, the second attempt should be made through minor punishments that are intended as *"eye-openers"* or *"convincers."* These punishments can be effective with naive risk-takers who need to be convinced that the state is serious about this matter (although they would not be effective with rational calculators who commit crimes with full awareness of the possible consequences of their actions). If *"convincer"* punishments fail, the system should embark on a program of *coerced treatment*. These treatments should be viewed in terms of their actual performance, of course, not just in terms of the good intentions of those who impose them. Finally, if coerced treatments fail, juveniles should be assumed to be rational calculators and waived to criminal court to receive *punishment* proportionate to their crimes.

Providing punishment for crimes therefore would NOT be a function of the juvenile court. This function would be carried out by the criminal court, and all youths who deserve such punishment would be transferred to criminal court to receive it there. The juvenile court would process only juveniles who are assumed to lack a clear understanding of the consequences of their actions. In terms of "criminal justice thermodynamics," the juvenile court would intentionally provide lenient penalties to assure that they are broadly applied.

Juvenile Justice Already Functions This Way

To a considerable extent, the juvenile justice system already functions this way, since it can be described as a graded sequence of escalating threats, convincer punishments, and coerced treatments. These are imposed by police, by intake and probation officers at the juvenile court, and by the juvenile court judge.

Police officers have their own sequence of escalating threats, convincer punishments, and coerced treatments that they routinely use when dealing with juvenile offenders.[20] Although they normally do not use the entire sequence with any particular juvenile, they can choose among the various steps in handling a particular case.

At the lowest level of the sequence, they "counsel and release" the youth—that is, tell the kid to beat it and not let it happen again. In practice, this involves a threat: If I see you again, then I will take more aggressive action.

At the next level, they may take the juvenile home to his or her parents without an arrest. At the next level, they may "station adjust" by bringing the juvenile to the police station and having the parents come down. At any of these levels, the police may throw in a "convincer" punishment or a coerced treatment: depending on the department, some officers require the juvenile to make restitution or write an essay or do some community service.

The next level of the sequence involves an official arrest but no referral to juvenile court. As always, this is accompanied by a threat: If I see you again, then I will make the referral. And finally, the police officer refers the case to juvenile court, at which point the system of escalating threats, convincer punishments, and coerced treatments is taken over by the juvenile probation officer.

Like police officers, juvenile probation officers can choose among a sequence of escalating threats, convincer punishments, and coerced treatments in deciding how to handle a particular case.[21] About half of the juveniles referred to juvenile court are handled entirely by the probation officer using this system and never see a judge.

At the lowest level of this sequence, the probation officer "counsels and releases" the youth without further action. This includes a threat: if you are referred to the court for another offense, I will file a petition not only on the new offense but also on this old offense as well.

At the next level of the sequence, the probation officer says the same thing but accompanies it with informal supervision or a formal consent decree (in which the juvenile and the parents sign a form agreeing to report to the probation officer for a certain period of time). These may involve some coerced treatment: a consent decree may require that the youth get some counseling or drug or alcohol treatment, or enroll in a vocational training school, and so on. It normally includes requirements that can be interpreted as minor punishments intended as "convincers"—obey curfew, report to the probation office once a week, and so on. It may include even more stringent punishments as "convincers"—perhaps a couple of days in the detention center,[22] or a certain amount of community service or restitution. These punishments are not intended to be proportionate to the offense, but to open the juvenile's eyes, to convince the juvenile that the state is serious about the matter. The final stage in the probation officer's sequence involves filing a petition to take the youth before the judge.

Like the police officer and the probation officer, the judge can choose from a sequence of escalating threats, convincer punishments, and coerced treatments in deciding how to handle a particular case.[23] The first level of the sequence involves withholding adjudication and ordering a consent decree. This is accompanied by a threat: If you come back to court, I will adjudicate you not only on the new offense but on this old offense as well.

The next level of the sequence involved adjudication and placement on formal probation. This disposition is normally accompanied by an explicit threat: If you are referred to the court again, I am going to remove you from your home. The next level involves removal from the home and placement in a community-based facility such as a foster or group home. After that, the judge can place the juvenile in a non-secure institutional setting and then in a secure institution. The final step in the entire juvenile justice process involves waiver to the criminal courts, where the juvenile would be expected to receive full punishment for the offense.

These stages are not clearly distinguished from each other, so another person might look at the same sequence and describe several more or several fewer stages. But as I describe it, police have five possible stages, probation officers four, and judges six. This means that there are somewhere around fifteen stages in the escalating sequence, beginning with a police "counsel and release" and ending with waiver to criminal court.

Few juveniles go through all stages. A juvenile whose first offense is very serious might be waived to criminal court despite having no prior record. A juvenile who commits many trivial offenses might be handled entirely by police officers and never be referred to juvenile court.

The point is that, in its present functioning, the juvenile justice system can be described as a graded system of escalating threats, convincer punishments, and coerced treatments. This system makes a lot of sense if its purpose is to communicate to naive risk-takers that actions have consequences. It makes no sense at all if its purpose is to punish hardened criminals for their offenses.

The Juvenile Justice System Is Highly Successful

The juvenile justice system successfully handles a large majority of the juveniles with whom it deals. This statement is supported by national statistics and various research studies on the distribution of juvenile cases.

Imagine 6,000 different situations in which the police encounter a juvenile who has committed an arrestable offense. On the average, this would involve about 2,000 different juveniles, so that the average juvenile who encounters the police does so in three different arrest situations.[24] About 1,000 of these juveniles will be arrested, some more than once, so that there will be about 2,000 official arrests in those 6,000 arrest situations.[25] In the situations in which there is no arrest, the juveniles will be counseled and released, taken home to their parents, or "station adjusted."

About 1,000 of these 2,000 arrests are handled on an informal basis by the police themselves,[26] and the remaining 1,000 arrests will be referred to the juvenile court for further action. The probation officer will handle approximately 507 of these cases without a formal court hearing, either with counsel and release, informal supervision, consent decree, and a few outright dismissals.[27]

About 9 cases will be transferred to criminal court. There will be about 484 disposition hearings, 460 without an adjudication hearing because the juveniles admit the offense and the other 24 with an adjudication, mostly because the juveniles deny the offense.[28] At the disposition hearing, about 282 of these youths will be placed on probation, 64 will be sent to a state or local institution, and 138 will receive a variety of other dispositions.

Defining "success" and "failure" in the juvenile justice system is to some extent a matter of opinion. But many people would define the 9 transfers to criminal court as failures of the system. These youths apparently ran through the entire sequence of escalating threats, convincer punishments, and coerced treatments, and continued to commit crimes. Assuming that these represent 9 different youths (so that no youth

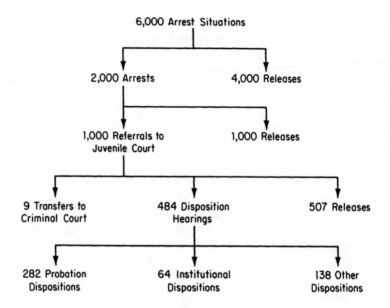

FIGURE 1. The Juvenile Justice "Funnel"

was transferred more than once), these are less than .5% of the 2,000 different juveniles who originally encountered the juvenile justice system. If they are the only failures, then the system has a 99.5% success rate.

The 64 juveniles sent to the institution also could be defined as failures. They reached the final stage of the system of threats, convincer punishments, and coerced treatments without dropping out of crime. Assuming these are 64 different juveniles (i.e., no juvenile was institutionalized more than once), these represent a little over 3% of the 2,000 juveniles handled by the system.

Counting 73 failures (64 institutionalizations and 9 transfers to criminal court) out of 2,000 different youths handled by the system, the juvenile justice system still has better than a 96% success rate. Actually, it is likely that at least some youths were institutionalized twice or that some of the institutionalized youth are later waived, so that there are fewer than 73 different youths. In that case, the success rate would be somewhat higher.

Although the argument gets extremely weak, the 282 probation dispositions could also be counted as failures. This would total 355 failures (9 transfers, 64 institutionalizations, and 282 probations) out of 2,000 different youths handled by the system. That would still leave the system with a 82% success rate. That is, 82% of the 2,000 different youths who were identified by police as having committed an average of three arrestable offenses were handled by the escalating system of threats, convincer punishments, and coerced treatments without so much as being placed on probation.

Of course, it is likely that the success rate is higher because of considerable overlap among these categories. Many youths are placed on probation more than once, or are later institutionalized or transferred to criminal court. Thus, there would be fewer than 355 different youths in this group. For example, if I estimated that 250 different youths received probation, institutionalization, or transfer, then the success rate would be 87.5%.[29]

The youths who are "successes" apparently drop out of the juvenile justice system because if they came back in, they would advance to the next stage and would appear in the statistics there. For example, juveniles who received informal probation would be expected to be formally adjudicated if they were arrested again. They would then be expected to receive at least formal probation as a disposition. That fact that there are a relatively small number of formal probation dispositions indicate that most of those who receive informal probation do not reappear in the system.

A separate question is whether these juveniles reappear in the adult system, having passed the age of 18. The question of age and persistence in criminality is presently entangled in a complex controversy involving longitudinal studies.[30] The specific issue relevant to this discussion, however, is not contested. There is virtually unanimous agreement that the proportion of all people involved in crime peaks at age 16 or 17 and then declines rapidly.[31] Given this widespread agreement, we can confidently expect that most juveniles who were involved in the juvenile justice system do not become further involved in the adult system.

This means that the juvenile justice system successfully handles the vast majority of juveniles with whom it comes into contact. These juveniles move into the graded system of escalating threats, convincer punishments, and coerced treatments. They apparently learn that actions have consequences and they stop committing offenses.

Why Does the System Appear to Be a Failure?

If the juvenile justice system has such a remarkable success rate, then why does it have a widespread image of failure? The answer is that most studies of juvenile justice examine only the failures of the system and ignore the successes. Having excluded all the successful cases, the studies conclude that the system is a failure.

In the above figures, there were 73 juveniles who were sent to the institution or waived to criminal court. While these were less than 4% of the total number of juveniles handled by the system, they were the clearest failures of the system. Many analyses of the juvenile justice system *begin with these juveniles who failed and trace their cases backwards* to the first contacts these youths had with police.

That is, they start with the set of juveniles who were institutionalized or waived to criminal court, and then evaluate the system solely on the basis of its performance with those youths. But these are the failures of the system, and so their cases necessarily demonstrate a history of failure. The juvenile encountered the police in an arrest situation but the police did not arrest. The juvenile later was arrested but was not referred to juvenile court. The juvenile later was arrested and referred to juvenile court but the probation officer handled the case informally. The juvenile later was arrested again and adjudicated but was placed on probation. Only after being repeatedly arrested and having "nothing" done is the juvenile finally sent to an institution or waived to criminal court. No wonder the juvenile justice system has such a bad reputation.

Such cases are real, but they are a tiny minority of all cases handled by the juvenile justice system. The vast majority use the leniency as an opportunity to refrain from committing further offenses. Thus, "nothing" is done (i.e., the juvenile is not institutionalized or transferred to criminal court) but the kid is never seen again. These are the successes of the system, but they are not included in many analyses precisely because they are handled in an informal manner and then they disappear. Thus, they are not as visible as juveniles who are handled in a formal manner and who keep returning.

In order to include successes as well as the failures, I *begin with all juveniles* who encounter the juvenile justice system *and trace their cases forward* to their outcomes, whether successful or unsuccessful. This includes the successes of the system as well as the failures.

Success cases vastly outnumber failure cases in the juvenile justice system. These are the juveniles whom the police could have arrested but did not, and who never have contact with the police again. These are the juveniles the police arrest but do not refer to the juvenile court, and who do not get into any more trouble. These are the juveniles who are referred to juvenile court but are handled informally by the probation officer, and are not referred to the court again. These are the juveniles whom the judge places on probation, and who successfully complete that probation with no further offenses.

The juvenile justice system has gotten a bum rap. Any criminal justice organization that successfully handles a vast majority of its cases ought to be considered an outstanding success. Instead, it is considered a failure by those who believe that any level of failure is unacceptable.

Reforming Juvenile Justice

The "idea of juvenile justice" as a system of communication using threats, convincer punishments, and coerced treatments is based on the actual performance of the existing juvenile justice system. Thus, it is not necessary to defend this idea against the argument made about earlier "ideas of juvenile justice": that the actual performance of the reform will not measure up to the good intentions of the reformers.

To a considerable extent, this "idea of juvenile justice" is not a reform at all, but a defense of the existing system against attacks of the "get tough" reformers. I believe those attacks only advance the cycle of juvenile justice, moving us along to an untenable position of the "forced choice" between harshly punishing and doing nothing at all. Once we get to that point, leniency will be reestablished in a new major reform. In my opinion, the most important thing at present is to break the cycle of juvenile justice by stopping the movement of the cycle toward greater toughness.

Reforming Juvenile Corrections: More Treatment

In an ideal world, however, I would move the system in the opposite direction, toward more treatment. Such reforms would not be based merely on my good intentions, but on research that evaluates the actual performance of these programs in the real world.

First, there is extensive evidence that a wide variety of individual treatment programs can substantially reduce juvenile crime.[32] For example, in the "Unified Delinquency Intervention Services" project, a variety of moderately well-run rehabilitation programs all reduced juvenile recidivism by about 50%.[33]

Second, the effectiveness of any individual treatment program is enhanced when it is embedded in a well-established network of other treatment programs.[34] This is probably because each program then is able to select only those juveniles who are most appropriate for its services, and to refer other juveniles to other programs. If a wide enough variety of programs are available, then an appropriate program can be found for almost every juvenile.

Third, the best way to develop and maintain such a broad network of well-established treatment services is by purchasing those services from private agencies rather than having state employees provide the services directly.[35] This allows free-market competition to enter the arena of juvenile corrections, so that better programs tend to flourish and worse programs tend to die. In contrast, the inertia that typically accompanies state-run programs usually prevents such a process.

Fourth, the vast majority of juvenile delinquents can be handled in a well-developed network of community services.[36] These services clearly are as effective as juvenile institutions at rehabilitating and reforming delinquents, and they probably are more effective.

Fifth, some serious juvenile offenders deserve serious punishment for their crimes, as argued by the "get tough" reformers. However, research suggests that handling these offenders in this way does not reduce their criminality in the future. Better results are obtained if these few serious offenders are placed in small, treatment-oriented, secure juvenile facilities.[37] These facilities reduce recidivism among the most serious juvenile offenders by up to 70%, and they are less expensive in the long run than simply sending these youths to prison.

Finally, there is no place in a modern juvenile justice system for large, custody-oriented juvenile institutions. So far as I can tell, the primary function of these institutions is to provide the public with a false sense of security that we are "getting tough" with delinquents. A second function is to provide jobs to state employees.[38] Neither of these functions would be maintained in an ideal juvenile justice system.

Reforming the Juvenile Court: The Right to Treatment

In connection with making juvenile corrections more treatment-oriented, I would provide juveniles with a constitutional right to treatment in the disposition hearing. This recommendation is derived from the logic of the Supreme Court's equal protection argument, which demands that juveniles actually receive treatment in the disposition hearing in order to offset the loss of due process rights in the adjudication hearing.

I argued above that juveniles have almost no due process rights in practice, in part because they have fewer rights to begin with, in part because they fail to exercise the rights they do have (especially the privilege against self-incrimination), and in part because the judge is free to adjudicate when there is reasonable doubt because of the unavailability of jury trials and appeals. As a result, almost all juveniles are found to have committed the offense for which they were referred to the juvenile court.

The absence of due process in the juvenile justice system should not be considered a failure of juvenile justice officials. Rather, it should be viewed as an inevitable consequence of dealing with juveniles who do not understand that actions have consequences. I have already said that there are two different meanings of this statement—juveniles may not understand the consequences criminal actions have for their victims in terms of injuries and death, and they may not understand the consequences criminal actions have for themselves in terms of punishments. Now I am asserting a third meaning of the same statement: juveniles may not understand the consequences of their failure to fully exercise their due process rights.

To the extent that the juvenile court deals with naive risk-takers, it should assume that these juveniles will not be able to fully exercise the formal due process rights they have been granted. This means that the denial of the law's equal protection in juvenile court cannot be remedied by the granting of formal due process rights. Instead, the juvenile court must achieve constitutionality by granting some compensating benefit that juveniles actually receive. The Supreme Court said that that was treatment, but it admitted that juveniles often do not actually receive treatment.

Several appellate courts have found that, because of the denial of equal protection, juveniles have a constitutional right to treatment in the juvenile court. In practice, this right means that juveniles who demonstrate that they are not receiving any treatment must be released from the jurisdiction of the court. The U.S. Supreme Court has never made such a ruling, although it has not made a contrary ruling either.[39]

I favor such a ruling with the understanding that juveniles who are fully able to exercise their due process rights should be waived to adult court where they can utilize them. Juvenile court, where the absence of due process would be balanced by a constitutional right to treatment, would then be limited to naive risk-takers.

This would restrict somewhat the power and flexibility of the state in disposition hearings. The focus of those hearings would be on coerced treatments, but threats and convincer punishments could be available if it was held that these were in the "best interests" of the juvenile. It would be unconstitutional, however, simply to punish juveniles for their offense. Juveniles who deserve such punishment would be waived to criminal court to receive it.

Good Intentions vs. Actual Performance

My recommendations for the reform of the juvenile justice system can be criticized by arguing that their actual performance would not live up to my good intentions. That certainly could be the outcome if these reforms were implemented. However, I would make three comments relevant to that subject.

First, I believe that there is sufficient research on the actual performance of community-based treatment-oriented juvenile corrections to conclude that they would work better than the institution-based systems that exist in most states. I would hope that other states follow the lead of Massachusetts, Utah, and Nebraska in creating such systems.

Second, in jurisdictions where judges have found a constitutional right to treatment, the impact on juvenile corrections has been favorable but has not resulted in a broad expansion of treatment services. Recommending a right to treatment therefore might seem idealistic.

However, I do not suggest that a constitutional right to treatment in itself would expand treatment in juvenile corrections. Such treatment networks must be created by state legislatures in the political process, as has already happened in three states. Once such a system is in place, then a constitutional right to treatment would act as a legal back-up to maintain it. In addition, the language of a constitutional right would keep the ideal of treatment in the forefront of juvenile corrections, helping to resist the tendency to slide into punishment and custody. Such a right also is required by the logic of the Supreme Court's equal protection argument and should exist strictly on its own merits.

Finally, I do not promise that my reforms would "solve" the problem of delinquency. In contrast, I state clearly that they would not, although I argue that such a system would work better then the present system. Since I promise less than most reformers, my reforms have a better chance of living up to my good intentions.

Would These Ideas Sell?

The four remaining "lessons of history" discuss characteristics of reforms that "sell" with the general public. Consider my ideas in relation to those lessons.

Reforms sell if they focus on changing the juvenile's behavior but do not require changes in anyone else's behavior, including rich and powerful people and juvenile justice bureaucrats. The ideas of juvenile delinquency and juvenile justice proposed here do not have such a focus. Like the Supreme Court's constitutional reform, these ideas promise a fair and reasonable method of responding to delinquents, but do not promise a "solution" to the problem of delinquency. In addition, the right to treatment in disposition hearings would require juvenile justice bureaucrats to change their behavior, and the establishment of a treatment-oriented correctional system would require state legislators to change their behavior. This suggests these ideas will not have much "sales appeal."

Reforms sell if they portray reformers as morally and intellectually superior to delinquents and their parents. The portrayal of delinquents as naive risk-takers suggests that adults are superior to juveniles in that adults know that actions have consequences. But that modest degree of superiority is insufficient to give this reform the kind of "sales appeal" found in earlier successful reforms, where delinquents were portrayed as potential paupers, dependent and neglected children, and hardened criminals.

Reforms sell when the reformers make an "unfair comparison," harshly assessing the actual performance of past policies but optimistically assessing future policies on the basis of their own good intentions. The product of this comparison is a promise to solve the problem of delinquency. I have not made such an unfair comparison here. In contrast, I have asserted that various policies must be fairly compared by looking at their actual performance. In addition, my recommendation is a policy that is already largely implemented. Thus, I cannot promise to solve the problem of delinquency. This reform therefore will have much less "sales appeal" than earlier successful reforms.

Finally, reforms sell when they expand the power of the state, based on the good intentions of the reformers and the optimistic promise to solve the problem of delinquency. But the only change in the juvenile justice system that I have recommended would restrict the power of the state: granting juveniles the right to treatment in disposition hearings. That right would mean the juvenile court would be required to act in the juvenile's best interests and could no longer simply punish juveniles for their offenses. If juveniles deserved punishment, they would have to receive it from criminal court.

I must conclude that my ideas have little "sales appeal." They simply do not tell people what they want to hear. Even if they would work in practice, they would not "make sense." Their chances of being implemented are poor.

Notes

1. See Bruce Bullington et al., "The Politics of Policy: Deinstitutionalization in Massachusetts 1970-1985," *Law & Policy* 8(4):507-14 (October, 1986).

2. Edward M. Murphy, "An Alternative Approach to Managing Juvenile Corrections," in Francis X. Hartmann, ed., *The Role of the Juvenile Court,* Springer-Verlag, New York, 1987, pp. 371-83.

3. Thomas J. Bernard and Daniel Katkin, "Introduction," *Law & Policy,* 8(4):391-95 (October, 1986).

4. See "Nebraska Legislature Begins Shift to Community Sanctions," *Criminal Justice Newsletter* 21(12):4-5 (June 15, 1990).

5. Richard J. Lundman, *Prevention and Control of Delinquency,* Oxford University Press, New York, 1984, Chapters 7, 8, 9.

6. Donna Hamparian, "Violent Juvenile Offenders," and Jeffrey L. Bleich, "Toward an Effective Policy for Handling Dangerous Juvenile Offenders," Chapters 9 and 10 in Hartmann, op. cit.

7. For overviews, see Parts I, II, and IV in James Q. Wilson and Glenn C. Loury, eds., *Families, Schools, and Delinquency Prevention,* Springer-Verlag, New York, 1987.

8. Bleich, op. cit., Hamparian, op. cit.

9. A frightening account of these offenders can be found in Clemens Bartollas, Stuart J. Miller, and Simon Dinitz, *Juvenile Victimization*, Sage, Beverly Hills, 1976.

10. Andrew Vachss and Yitzak Bakel, *The Life-Style Violent Juvenile*, Lexington Books, Lexington, MA, 1979, p. 9.

11. E.g., thirty-five years after the Cambridge-Somerville study, Joan McCord ("Consideration of Some Effects of a Counseling Program," in S. E. Martin, L. B. Sechrest, and R. Redner, eds., *New Directions in the Rehabilitation of Criminal Offenders*, National Academy Press, Washington, D.C., 1981) found that 68% of the control group (i.e., those who had received no special treatment) had not died, been convicted of an index offense, or diagnosed as alcoholic, schizophrenic, or manic-depressive. See also Marvin E. Wolfgang, Terence P. Thornberry, and Robert M. Figlio, *From Boy to Man*, University of Chicago Press, Chicago, 1987, for a follow-up on the Philadelphia birth cohort.

12. E.g., see Robert G. Wahler, "Contingency Management with Oppositional Children," in Wilson and Loury, op. cit., pp. 112–31.

13. Philip J. Cook and John H. Laub, "Trends in Child Abuse and Juvenile Delinquency," in Hartmann, op. cit., pp. 110–12.

14. See, e.g., Curt Bartol and Anne Bartol, *Juvenile Delinquency*, Prentice-Hall, Englewood Cliffs, 1989.

15. In general, see John Hagan, *Structural Criminology*, Rutgers University Press, New Brunswick, NJ, 1989, pp. 153–58.

16. This image is consistent with the most popular and broadly supported theory of delinquency: Travis Hirschi, *Causes of Delinquency*, University of California Press, Berkeley, 1969. My own objections to this theory concern what I call here the "rational calculators." In general, I have argued that a structural explanation is more appropriate for these offenders. See Thomas J. Bernard, "Structure and Control," *Justice Quarterly* 4(3):409–24 (September, 1987), and George B. Vold and Thomas J. Bernard, *Theoretical Criminology*, Oxford University Press, New York, 1986, Chapter 13.

17. Charles A. Murray and Louis A. Cox, Jr., *Beyond Probation*, Sage, Beverly Hills, 1979.

18. E.g., see Joel Samaha, *Criminal Law*, West, St. Paul, 1983, pp. 52–75. In particular, see the Model Penal Code reprinted there, which distinguishes between purposely, knowingly, recklessly, or negligently committing crime. Each is defined in terms of awareness of consequences.

19. See James Q. Wilson, *Thinking About Crime*, Basic, New York, 1985.

20. See, e.g., George L. Kelling, "Juveniles and Police," in Hartmann, op. cit., pp. 203–18.

21. See, for example, William A. Reese, II, Russell L. Curtis, Jr., and Albert Richard, Jr., "Juvenile Justice as People-Modulating," *Journal of Research in Crime and Delinquency* 26(4):329–57 (November, 1989); and Michael W. Oshima and Francis X. Hartmann, "Juvenile Justice in Transition: An Industry Note," in Hartmann, op. cit., pp. 308–26.

22. See Paul Lerman, *Community Treatment and Social Control*, University of Chicago Press, Chicago, 1975.

23. See Paul N. Weingart, "Classifying Juvenile Dispositions," in Hartmann, op. cit., pp. 329–48.

24. E.g., in the Philadelphia birth cohort study, about 3,500 different juveniles accounted for about 10,000 contacts with the police. It is not very meaningful to describe the "average" offender, since over half of these youths had only a single contact while other youths had as many as thirty-five. See Thomas J. Bernard and R. Richard Ritti, "The Philadelphia Birth Cohort and Selective Incapacitation," *Journal of Research in Crime and Delinquency*, 28:33–54 (Feb., 1991).

25. In the Philadelphia birth cohort study, about one-third of police contacts resulted in arrest. This is a high figure, however, since only 15% of police contacts resulted in arrest in Donald J. Black and Albert J. Reiss, "Police Control of Juveniles," *American Sociological Review* 35:63–67 (1970) (see also Black's "The Social Organization of Arrest," *Stanford Law Review* 23:1087–1111 1971), and only 16% of police contacts resulted in arrest in Richard J. Lundman et al., "Police Control of Juveniles: A Replication," *Journal of Research in Crime and Delinquency* 16:74–91 (1979). Taking the lower figure found in these studies would increase the "success rate" that is computed for the juvenile justice system. None of these studies provides clear data on the number of different juveniles involved in these arrests, so I estimated that. See also Robert M. Terry, "Discrimination in the Handling of Juvenile Offenders by Social Control Agencies," *Journal of Research in Crime and Delinquency* 4:218–230 (1967).

26. Kelling, op. cit.; Cook and Laub, op. cit.

27. Cook and Laub, op. cit., p. 111. Their data is based on H. N. Snyder, T. A. Finnegan, and J. L. Hutzler, *Delinquency 1981*. National Center for Juvenile Justice, Pittsburgh, 1983.

28. H. Ted Rubin, *Juvenile Justice*, Random House, New York, 1985; Rubin, "The Juvenile Court Landscape," in Albert R. Roberts, *Juvenile Justice*, Dorsey, Chicago, 1989, p. 129.

29. In addition, the success rate would be higher if a lower proportion of police contacts results in arrest. See note 25.

30. See, e.g., the first five articles in *Criminology* 26(1) (February, 1988).

31. For a review, see David P. Farrington, Lloyd E. Ohlin, and James Q. Wilson, *Understanding and Controlling Crime*, Springer-Verlag, New York, 1986, Chapter 2. The controversy concerns whether the remaining "active" criminals continue to commit crime at a high rate, or whether their rate of offending declines with age.

32. For a review, see Paul Gendreau and Robert R. Ross, "Revivification of Rehabilitation: Evidence from the 1980s," *Justice Quarterly* 4(3):349–407 (Sept., 1987).

33. Charles A. Murray and Louis A. Cox, Jr., *Beyond Probation*, Sage, Beverly Hills, 1979. The results of this study often are interpreted to mean that institutional corrections are more effective than community corrections. That interpretation overlooks the major point of the book, which is emphasized by its title—one can achieve major reductions in recidivism once one gets beyond simple probation.

34. Robert B. Coates, Alden D. Miller, and Lloyd E. Ohlin, *Diversity in a Youth Correctional System*, Ballinger, Cambridge, MA, 1978.

35. Murphy, op. cit.

36. Lundman, op. cit.

37. Bleich, op. cit.

38. See the response of government employees to the threatened closing of institutions in Illinois in Kenneth Wooden, *Weeping in the Playtime of Others*, McGraw-Hill, New York, 1976.

39. For a review, see Rubin, op. cit., 1985, Chapter 7.

10

The End of Juvenile Delinquency

Juveniles always have committed more than their share of crime, and the lessons of history suggest that this will not change. Thus, there is a sense in which the problem of juvenile delinquency cannot be solved because, in one way or another, it is a permanent and unchanging product of human nature.

But the modern problem of delinquency, as urban property crime by lower-class youths, appeared in Western Europe and America about two hundred years ago in connection with the birth of the modern, urban, industrialized world. As other nations have gone through the same modernization process since then, the same modern problem of juvenile delinquency appeared in them. Because this modern problem of delinquency appeared at some point in the past, it can also disappear at some point in the future. Thus, there is a sense in which the problem of juvenile delinquency actually can be "solved."

Solving that problem cannot be accomplished merely by introducing a new juvenile justice policy. Rather, it requires changing the larger social conditions that gave rise to the problem in the first place. New York City in 1825 did not have a wave of juvenile delinquency because it had an inadequate juvenile justice system. Neither did Chicago in 1899. Those waves of delinquency occurred because of the larger social conditions associated with modernization, urbanization, and industrialization. In the language of the time, it was neither the "peculiar weaknesses of the children's moral natures," or their "weak and criminal parents," but the "manifold temptations of the streets" that were the source of the problem.

In both New York and Chicago, changing those social conditions was one possible response to the new problem of juvenile delinquency, but the reformers of the time ignored that possibility and focused instead on changing the behavior of juvenile delinquents and their parents. This response was chosen because it would have been very inconvenient to attempt to change the social conditions under which poor people lived.

Today, we continue to attempt to change the behavior of juvenile delinquents and their parents because it is so inconvenient for us to attempt to change larger social conditions. Yet ultimately those conditions are the origin of the problem of delinquency, and changing them is the only way to solve that problem.

Traditional societies lacked a problem of juvenile delinquency because juveniles in them were firmly embedded in a larger social context. They were born into a fixed place in society, and moved from childhood through adolescence and into adulthood with a clear understanding of the roles they would play and the functions they would have in the larger society.

Such a firm embedding is not inconsistent with modern, urban, industrialized societies. European countries that have well-developed apprenticing programs for youths have lower delinquency rates.[1] Many middle- and upper-class youths in our own society also have a firm sense of being on a clear track that moves from childhood through adolescence and into an adulthood in which they will have a role and a function. Research suggests that such juveniles do not engage in juvenile delinquency.[2]

Juveniles who engage in delinquency, however, often lack just such a sense of having a role and place in the larger society. This is particularly true for juveniles in the lowest social classes, who are "left out" of meaningful roles. Such youths live in conditions that can generate extreme kinds of violent behavior.[3] Until such conditions are changed, we should expect to continue to have a serious problem with juvenile delinquency.

I doubt that we will choose to make the social changes that would be required to solve the problem of delinquency because they would be very expensive. However, I also believe that modern societies will continue to evolve in a direction of increasing complexity and structural integration, gradually incorporating into meaningful roles more and more of those who are presently "left out."[4]

Thus, although I do not believe that we will ever "solve" the problem of delinquency, I do expect that it will someday "end." At that point, people will look back on the several hundred year history of juvenile delinquency and see it as a historically bounded phenomenon, like witchcraft in the Middle Ages[5] or the violence of the American "Wild West."[6] We will have a sense of its beginning at a certain historical point and ending at a certain historical point, and its relationship to the broader social and economic conditions in society at the time.

In the meantime, I hope that we give up the idea that the problem of juvenile delinquency can be solved by making changes in the juvenile justice system, since that idea leads only to the cycle of juvenile justice. Let us choose juvenile justice policies on the basis of their actual performance, not on the good intentions of those who favor those policies. Let us establish a fair, reasonable, and stable juvenile justice policy that responds to a problem that it does not create and cannot eliminate.

Finally, let us admit that we choose to live with the problem of juvenile delinquency because it is less costly and more convenient than choosing to solve it. That being the case, I hope we stop describing delinquents and their parents as morally and intellectually inferior to the rest of us. Let us respond to delinquents in the spirit of the founders of the first juvenile court: as firm but kindly parents. We cannot ignore delinquent behavior, but we must not forget that to some extent it is the result of our own choices. Conscious of our own failings, let us be more gentle with the failings of these juveniles.

Notes

1. David Greenberg, *Crime and Capitalism,* Mayfield, Palo Alto, 1981, pp. 64–66. These are introductory comments to Greenberg's article "Delinquency and the Age Structure of Society," *Contemporary Crises* 1:189–223 (April, 1977), reprinted on pp. 118–39 of his book.

2. In theoretical terms, these juveniles are controlled by "commitment," the rational investment in conformity and the risks of losing that investment through delinquency. See Travis Hirschi, *Causes of Delinquency,* University of California Press, Berkeley, 1969;

and Thomas J. Bernard, "Structure and Control: Reconsidering Hirschi's Concept of Commitment," *Justice Quarterly* 4(3):409–24 (September, 1987).

3. E.g., Thomas J. Bernard, "Angry Aggression Among the 'Truly Disadvantaged,' " *Criminology* 28(1):73–96 (February, 1990).

4. This is basically a Durkheimian view of the evolution of societies. See Emile Durkheim, *The Division of Labor in Society,* Free Press, New York, 1965. A traditional Marxist view would hold the opposite: as capitalist societies evolve, more and more people are "left out," ultimately resulting in a violent overthrow of the established order.

5. E.g., Elliott P. Currie, "Crimes Without Criminals," *Law and Society Review* 3(1):7–32 (August, 1968).

6. Eric H. Monkkonen, ed., *Crime and Justice in American History,* Meckler, Westport, CT, 1990, vol. 4.

Index

Printed in the United States
144901LV00002B/6/P

9 780195 071832